D1611182

CITY FOREST
MUMBAI'S NATIONAL PARK

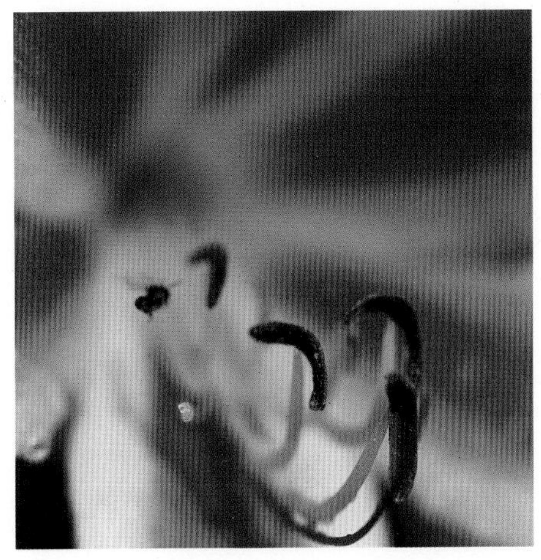

All photographs by Sunjoy Monga except where otherwise indicated

ISBN 81-7508-297-6
First published 2000

Design &
Digital Image Enhancement
F X DESIGNS

Processing
REPROSCAN

Printing
PRAGATI ART PRINTERS

Published by
INDIA BOOK HOUSE LIMITED
412 Tulsiani Chambers
Nariman Point
Mumbai 400 021
ibhpub@vsnl.com

This book is printed on 100% recycled paper

CITY FOREST
MUMBAI'S NATIONAL PARK

Text & Photographs
SUNJOY MONGA

Foreword
HUMAYUN ABDULALI

INDIA BOOK HOUSE LIMITED

I went to the woods because I wished to live deliberately,
to front only the essential facts of life,
and see if I could not learn what it had to teach, and not,
when I came to die, discover that I had not lived.
– Henry David Thoreau

The publisher gratefully acknowledges the generous support of the Godrej group of companies

He came in quietly at the meetings of the many causes he espoused, the symbolic black ribbon on his sleeve a deliberate reminder of his personal distress at the unsatisfactory state of the country, in particular matters he felt needed public attention. Though his entry was never conspicuous, his observations and viewpoints – his very presence – always made an impression, such was his characteristically low-key magnetism. His comments reflected his sincere and deeply-held beliefs, revealing the patron of several causes. S P Godrej, affectionately known as Sohrabji, late Chairman of the Godrej group of companies, was among the last of the great nationalists, a high-thinking, down-to-earth gentleman of wide-ranging interests. Archaeology and heritage conservation, the arts, education, the environment, international affairs, population control and development, scientific management, social welfare – he was ardent about each one of them, and integrated his social responsibility with business and industry long before it became a corporate cliché. Sohrabji was the recipient of several awards for the direction and support to the causes he stood for, and was conferred the Padma Bhushan by the President of India in 1999, as well as the 25th Anniversary Benefactors Award by the World Wide Fund for Nature.

Awards did not matter to Sohrabji. His philosophy was to strive to make the best of one's innate abilities and to cultivate a logical scientific temper. He deplored a lethargic, fatalistic attitude, lamenting the lack of rational ethos. Humane and humble, he treated one and all with equal respect. While most remember him for his concern and fondness for the environment and wildlife, Sohrabji was also amongst the foremost champions of population stabilisation. He strongly asserted that population growth and environmental issues were closely interrelated, and that only a balance between population and resources could enhance the quality of existence.

Sohrabji's concerns encompassed both immediate and long-term issues, but he laced his seriousness with a dry sense of humour. In the 1980s, I made several visits to Pirojshanagar – the sprawling Godrej township in Mumbai's eastern suburb of Vikhroli – along with his nephew, Rishad Naoroji. When we presented Sohrabji with a list of the 128 bird species we observed there, he quipped, "I didn't realise we have more birds than products here!" He was delighted to notice a huge colony of nesting cormorants, egrets and night herons in one of the industrial plants. He phoned me excitedly one morning with the news that the fledglings of White-throated Fantails nesting outside his bedroom window had taken their first flight. He always found time for such 'little' interests amid his colossal commitments, and he was keenly aware that biodiversity must be preserved not for what we get from it but what would happen if we were to lose it.

"The struggle between urgent demands to sustain our rising numbers and lasting conservation interests is only getting more intense. To check this, we will have to change our act – education of children and emancipation of women hold answers; industry will have to get more proactive on the environmental front," he remarked while driving through Mumbai's national park, on World Forestry Day only a few weeks before his death. Sohrabji had coined a slogan, "Save Mumbai to help India", and linked this with Mahatma Gandhi's quote, "Each of us must be the change we wish to see in the world." This book on Mumbai's forest, a peerless wilderness that he so cherished, is a tribute to the philosophy of this great man.

I dedicate this work to the memory of S P Godrej, our Sohrabji.

Sunjoy Monga

CONTENTS

FOREWORD

I have known the area around Kanheri Caves since my school days in the 1920s. I would catch a train to Borivli and then walk or cycle along a dirt road through the dense forest. Locals would warn me to be careful of tigers and leopards – sadly, I never saw a single tiger. But the forest, my introduction to ornithology, had a fascinating bird life and I collected some birds for St. Xavier's College, Mumbai. Several years of travel and collections in the forest resulted in a book, *Birds of Bombay and Salsette*, which I co-authored with the late Dr Salim Ali. Unfortunately, all of that bird collection has now vanished, and with it many ecological and general notes that I had made on the specimen labels. The earliest written notes I retain of my numerous visits to the forests date from January 1, 1940.

In 1940, I was elected to the Executive Committee of the Bombay Natural History Society (BNHS) and became its Honorary Secretary in 1947. This brought me in contact with government officers of the forest and various other departments. I made constant efforts to ensure that the large wilderness – stretching north of Aarey Milk Colony, through the catchment areas of Vihar Lake and Tulsi Lake and continuing further to Kanheri Caves and beyond – be declared a national park to be preserved in its entirety. This was finally agreed to by the central government in the early 1960s and the area was declared a national park.

In 1975, the authorities realised that a road through the park, connecting Goregaon to Mulund, would shorten the distance from the city's western suburbs to Nasik, Pune and beyond. Little time was wasted and work began on the road that would run diagonally through the centre of the national park, between the lakes. Many individuals and associations protested, some even sent representations to the central government. It was the year of the Emergency and Indira Gandhi was in no mood to listen to reason.

Having been associated with this forest for nearly half a century and aware of the havoc this road would cause in the entire national park – the heavy traffic that would pass through, bringing in its wake repair shops and hotels – I decided to act, come what may. With the assistance of Atul Setalvad and other distinguished lawyers, and a few members of the BNHS including Murad Fyzee and B Basu, we managed to secure a stay order from the Bombay High Court. The work on the road was halted. A few years later, the government tried restarting the project, with no success. This was a national park and its limits could not be changed without the consent of both the houses of parliament. A simple legal tool had been used effectively.

There is no doubt that this is a very special forest. Leopard, Sambar, Chital, Barking Deer, many other mammals, over 275 species of birds, and so much more, all exist within and immediately around the city's limits. One hopes that today's forest officers will continue to protect the forest and its wildlife with the dedication and expertise of the traditional *shikari* huntsmen. The heart and lungs of Mumbai, the park is an ideal escape from the lung-burning pollution and traffic jams of the dehumanising and overcrowded city, barely a few minutes from this pristine wilderness.

This absorbing book, with its beautiful pictures and informative text, will introduce the layman to the biodiversity that exists in this forest that is "the city's backyard". For the past seventy years, I've witnessed the continual degradation of Mumbai city and it is disheartening to see how this deterioration has impinged upon the pristine world of the national park, particularly over the last two decades. *City Forest: Mumbai's National Park* should go a long way towards making people realise the importance of preserving this forest for the present and the future.

Humayun Abdulali
Emeritus Naturalist – BNHS

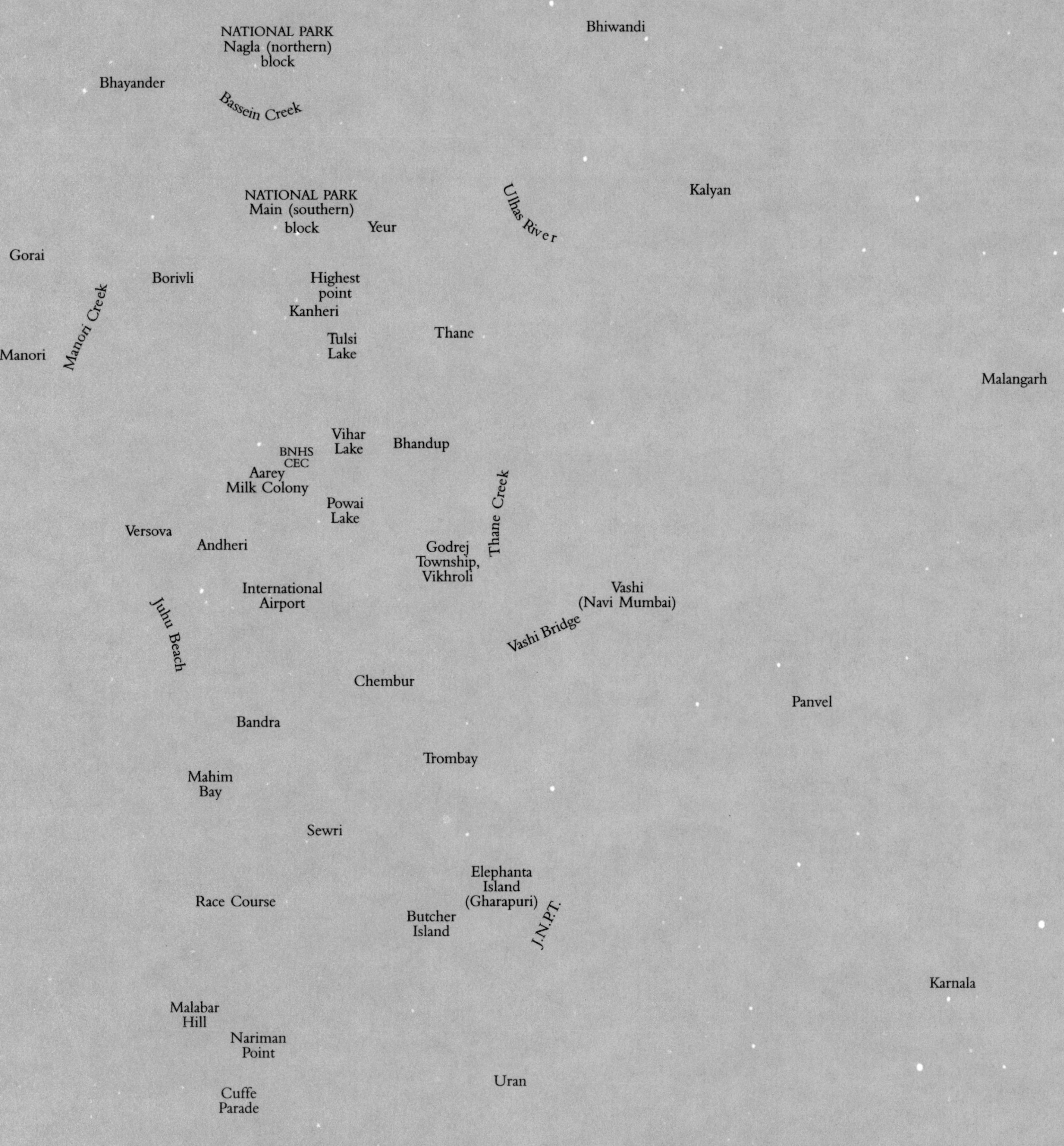

Satellite image courtesy National Remote Sensing Agency (NRSA), Hyderabad.

Forests of
Thane district

Bhiwandi

NATIONAL PARK
Nagla (northern)
block

Bhayander

Bassein Creek

Kalyan

Ulhas River

NATIONAL PARK
Main (southern)
block

Yeur

Gorai

Borivli

Highest
point

Kanheri

Manori Creek

Thane

Tulsi
Lake

Manori

Malangarh

Vihar
Lake

Bhandup

BNHS
CEC

Aarey
Milk Colony

Thane Creek

Powai
Lake

Versova

Andheri

Godrej
Township,
Vikhroli

Vashi
(Navi Mumbai)

International
Airport

Matheran

Vashi Bridge

Juhu Beach

Chembur

Panvel

Bandra

Trombay

Mahim
Bay

Sewri

Elephanta
Island
(Gharapuri)

Race Course

Butcher
Island

J.N.P.T.

Karnala

Malabar
Hill

Nariman
Point

Uran

Cuffe
Parade

Dharamtar Creek

Satellite image courtesy National Remote Sensing Agency (NRSA), Hyderabad.

INTRODUCTION

Lying in the northern part of Mumbai, the Sanjay Gandhi National Park is an oasis in the midst of lifeless concrete and teeming crowds. Perhaps no other megalopolis can boast of such a spectacular array of nature's sights – dark, volcanic rocks on top of the ancient Buddhist caves of Kanheri, the enchanting Jambulmal summit, the tranquil Tulsi Lake, the dramatic expanse around Vihar Lake, the slopes of the bird-rich Pongam Valley and the tangle of Karvi growth.

My fascination with this peerless wilderness began on an August morning in 1969 when I first visited the park as a young boy. It was the monsoon season and the forest was lush and dark. Splashing in a forest stream turgid with rainwater, I suddenly saw a snake swimming towards me. Petrified, I broke into a run, screaming, and injured my toe. Moments later, I saw my first wild peafowl with his glorious tail fanned out and my bruised toe was forgotten. I swung on a rope-like vine and was dwarfed by an oversized leaf. I saw glorious flowers and a troop of playful monkeys. I was hooked.

Fortunate to be living only a few minutes drive from the park, I found myself going back again and again. My father was very supportive of my fascination with the forest and over the next few years I made several trips to the park. Discouraged from crossing the railway tracks and venturing into the wilderness on my own, I was initially only allowed to explore the countryside surrounding our home – a verdant world of orchards and paddy fields, of birds, snakes and mongooses. A few hundred metres from our house, a rivulet flowed from the hills to the east. In the monsoon, these forested hills would be enveloped in mist and covered with a green carpet of shrubs, ferns and fungi, and snake-like creepers would be wrapped around the trees.

During one of my rambles in this countryside, I met Joslin Rodrigues, who proved to be a remarkable companion. Joslin succeeded – after repeated warnings against climbing trees, catching snakes and straying too deep into the forest – in persuading my mother to allow me to go into the forest with him. From early 1972, we made more than 400 trips to the park. During the ten long and enjoyable years of discovery we learned more about the forest than we could ever have from the confines of a classroom or the pages of a book.

The summer of 1976 was particularly eventful. It was early June and the monsoon was yet to break in full force. Joslin had climbed a leafy tree and as he jumped down, a car screeched to a halt. At the wheel was an elderly gentleman, accompanied by a charming, elderly lady. "What are you doing here?" he inquired, looking at us with his penetrating eyes. "And what are you hiding?" he asked Joslin, who sheepishly stretched out his hand to reveal an abandoned iora's nest we had pilfered. Later, we showed the gentleman the nest of a long-tailed, black bird – the Greater Racket-tailed Drongo, he was quick to inform us. He then generously invited us to accompany him to Vihar Lake where he set up a few field chairs and whipped out a large thermos flask of steaming tea. Little did I know then of the long hours I was destined to spend with the renowned ornithologist Humayun Abdulali and his grand thermos.

That hour on the grassy margins of Vihar Lake deepened my interest in nature study and the national park. Some weeks later, I visited the Bombay Natural History Society (BNHS), where the venerable Humayun Abdulali and the late J S Serrao, a naturalist, showed me the society's bird collection. Over the years, I have accompanied Abdulali on more than a hundred memorable bird-watching trips in this park and elsewhere.

Frequent visits to the park have helped me appreciate its wealth of biodiversity. Mumbai's spectacular field laboratory, this forest is a great educator of natural history and conservation. It isn't surprising that Mumbai has a growing number of environmentally conscious citizens, bird-watchers, plant and butterfly enthusiasts, and trekkers – all with a special love and concern for this wilderness. My own passion for the natural world might not have been so intense had it not been for the accessibility of this park. I have visited many forests since my early trips to Mumbai's national park, but this wilderness retains a special place in my heart.

Today, the dark rocks of Kanheri remain as dramatic as in 1969, but much has changed in the landscape around the park. The almost village-like suburban north Mumbai, visible from the rocky ridges, has now transformed into a concrete jungle of apartment blocks, slums and gas-belching industrial sprawls. The forest barely ends before the shanty towns, residential and industrial complexes begin. More than half a million people live and work in the slums and quarries bordering the park and thousands spill over into forest land. Encroachment is one of the park's major problems. However, inside the park, it is still a rugged, wild world. No other metropolis with over 30,000 people packed to a square kilometre has, within its city limits, a peerless forest quite like this one.

PEERLESS

W I L D E R N E S S

The Sanjay Gandhi National Park, sandwiched between Mumbai's western and eastern suburbs, is the city's backyard. In an overcrowded metropolis where open spaces are vanishing and real estate prices are among the highest in the world, the park's survival is nothing short of a miracle. The forest, extending over an area of 86.96 sq km in the Mumbai and Thane districts of Western Maharashtra, is a sanctuary for a wealth of biodiversity.

Tigers are said to have roamed the forest trails below Kanheri Hill until the early twentieth century. I remember Joslin's father, Joseph Rodrigues, telling us how he once saw a tiger in the early 1920s while driving livestock to graze on the verdant slopes. The last authentic record of a tiger's presence was of one shot on the edge of Vihar Lake on January 22, 1929. But according to Rodrigues the tiger probably survived in these forests till 1940. Today, the great striped cat has been re-imported into the park and can only be seen in the tiger safari enclosure.

Not much has been documented on the tiger's presence in the park, but the 1882 *Bombay Gazetteer* (Thana district) has some interesting anecdotes of tigers in this region: "About a century ago (1774), the Sálsette [formerly a large island in the northern part of Bombay including the area that is now the national park] hills were infested with tigers who came freely down to the plains." A hundred years later in "the five years ending 1879 fifty-three human beings and 935 head of cattle were killed by tigers. During the same period ninety-nine tigers were slain." At that time, tigers were without adequate protection and it was feared that the species might vanish if appropriate measures were not taken.

M G Gogate, former Chief Wildlife Warden of Maharashtra state, explains that this forest – lying in the Malabar Coast region of the Western Ghat biogeographic zone – is gifted with a rich biodiversity, though large animals like the tiger and the Indian Bison or Gaur have now vanished. "Interestingly, there was a report of a Gaur found fifteen years ago in the Shahpur forest, barely 40 km from the national park as the crow flies. Perhaps this was a captive animal as it appears highly improbable for a Gaur to be inhabiting the forest today," he informs.

I also gathered information from Gogate on the early history of this forested region. The existing park is an interesting mosaic of government reserve lands, *inam* lands (granted by local rulers to loyal subjects) and lands specially acquired between 1860-75 for the creation of the Tulsi and Vihar water reservoirs. During 1937-42, the Bombay Municipal Corporation acquired the catchment areas of the two lakes and at a later date, lands belonging to the Aarey Milk Colony, a government dairy southwest of the park. In 1950, under the Bombay National Park Act, the Krishnagiri National Park was established with an area of about 20 sq km. In September 1968, a decision to create the Borivli National Park, roughly covering an area of 68.27 sq km, was taken. In 1969, an independent forest sub-division was created, giving the park a special status. Subsequently, in 1981, the park was renamed Sanjay Gandhi National Park. Over the years, the area was extended with the inclusion of forest tracts in the adjacent Thane division and the acquisition of some adjoining private lands.

TOP: *View of a residential complex near the western periphery of the park.*

BOTTOM: *Lithograph of Tiger with Baby, engraved by Chs Heath. Scene of a melancholy event on the island of Salsette.*

The park is almost two hours by road from the humdrum world of south Mumbai, the commercial hub of the city. It takes about thirty minutes to reach the park from the international airport. Daytime descents into Mumbai reveal an aerial panorama – the aircraft flies over or alongside a hilly, green carpet before concrete structures and sprawling slums take over. From air, the contrast between the verdant, hilly expanse of the forest and the chaotic, congested city is striking. On land it is even more apparent. It takes barely ten minutes to escape from the snarled suburban Mumbai into the pristine wilderness of the park.

A staff photographer with the Indian Navy, Gopal Bodhe, who has done extensive aerial photography over coastal India recounts his experience of flying over this forest. "I couldn't believe it. Within ten minutes of taking off in a helicopter from the tip of south Mumbai we were over what could've been some remote forest dotted with lakes. But a slight turn of the head and I could see the city," exclaims Bodhe, who has been to the park many times in the last thirty years but finds this aerial view the most mesmerising.

The park lies to the west of the Western Ghat mountain range and flanks India's extensive westerly seaboard. Mumbai's national park lies at the northern tip of a biologically rich region that experiences heavy rainfall. The main hill ranges here generally run north to south with small offshoots to the west and east. Low-lying areas can be seen around Vihar Lake and in the tourism zone towards the main entrance of the park. The elevation ranges from near sea level at Bassein Creek – frequented by multitudes of waders, gulls and terns – to a height of 486 m, the park's highest point.

From a high-rise apartment overlooking the park, I can survey the horizon in a sweep – from the creek, nearly four kilometres to the west, to the satellite tower on the park's highest point, four kilometres to the east. The attraction of several residential complexes here is their proximity to the forest. A promontory on the summit plateau has one of the most spectacular views and I sit here for hours, observing birds of prey – buzzards, eagles, falcons and vultures. I once saw nine species of birds in just two hours, soaring on the thermals, some occasionally swishing close. Every few months some of us trek to this point just to breathe in the cool refreshing air so rare in Mumbai.

TOP: *Forested hills, seen from a high-rise apartment near the park.*

BOTTOM: *Dense vegetation covers the park's eastern hills.*

From this little headland, the great expanse of the forested valley can be seen edged by hills to the east and west. Nestled in the folds of the valley are the two lakes, Tulsi and Vihar, like mirrors in the landscape. Sometimes, Powai, Mumbai's third lake, is also visible. A large mass of water, it lies outside the area of the park of which the far-end of Vihar Lake forms the southern boundary. The park's highest point, lying above Kanheri Caves, is enchanting during the monsoon when it is often enveloped in a veil of mist that occasionally lifts to reveal the landscape. The summit and the gentle slopes around are covered with tall Karvi growth. Towards the end of the rains, between September and October, ground orchids are in bloom. The hilltop is full of inspiring sights and a trek to this point is a voyage of discovery, a revelation of nature's changing hues.

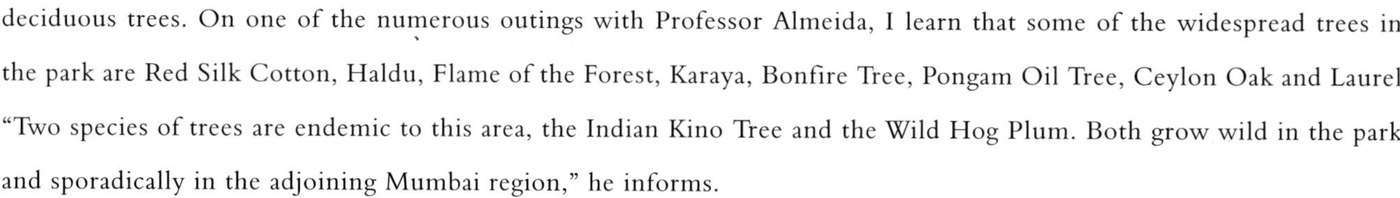

The park is predominantly a mixed-deciduous forest. An excursion with the eminent botanist, Professor M R Almeida, is a rewarding experience and Mumbai's botany enthusiasts look forward to this annual monsoon walk organised by the Bombay Natural History Society (BNHS). He informs us that there are nearly 800 flowering species here, including trees, herbs and grasses. "We do not as yet have a clear picture of the number of non-flowering species," he says. I asked him to hazard a guess. After much consideration he estimated that there must be at least a thousand, chiefly fungi and algae. "There are some tree species that have as many as five fungal associates but unfortunately we do not have a complete database on the forest's rich biodiversity, despite its incredibly easy accessibility," informs Professor Almeida.

There are stretches where teak is the dominant tree but such areas are not extensive and much of the terrain is covered with many other deciduous trees. On one of the numerous outings with Professor Almeida, I learn that some of the widespread trees in the park are Red Silk Cotton, Haldu, Flame of the Forest, Karaya, Bonfire Tree, Pongam Oil Tree, Ceylon Oak and Laurel. "Two species of trees are endemic to this area, the Indian Kino Tree and the Wild Hog Plum. Both grow wild in the park and sporadically in the adjoining Mumbai region," he informs.

The forest has a distinct character in each season. During the monsoon it is luxuriant and mystical. When it pours I remain relatively dry under a canopy of leaves that serves as an umbrella. My senses are alert and I feel dwarfed and lost amid the floral abundance. Nature's design is marvellous. The foliage tames the raw power of the falling rain and water drops trickle down to the forest floor, gently and impartially penetrating the life-sustaining soil. Nothing is wasted. The dead are returned to the soil; the work of countless life forms, aided by different kinds of fungi, including the enchanting mushrooms.

TOP: *Habenaria Orchid in bloom at the park's highest point.*

BOTTOM: *A gushing stream along the Silonda trail.*

For a few short weeks during the rains the forest streams come to life, bubbling and occasionally roaring in the wake of a torrential downpour. The gushing, winding stream along the Silonda trail is fascinating and to be here at the height of the monsoon is like being transported to a remote wilderness. Never do I feel more distant from the suffocating city than when I stand by the streams deep within this forest, absorbing their flowing rhythm.

Scattered patches of evergreen trees can usually be seen along watercourses, in some valleys and intermittently along hill slopes. The dominant tree among them is the Ashoka. At the very top of the Jambulmal summit, and on an adjoining mountain-top, the bluish flowers of the Iron Wood Tree are visible. The most extensive stretch of such a forest is around and above Kanheri Caves but the total extent is less than 20 hectares. On the slopes and in the lower reaches there are some fruit-bearing trees like Black Plum and Mango Tree and also several species of *Ficus*.

The trek to the highest point in the park passes through a patch of evergreen forest. It is always dark under the Ashoka trees and there is a distinct drop in temperature. I feel a crispness and gentle radiance in the air. The harmonious notes of the Malabar Whistling Thrush and White-rumped Shama, the rich but wavering song of the Brown-cheeked Fulvetta and the chatter of a Bonnet Macaque troop add to the ambience. One of the massive mango trees here once housed a pair of Jungle Owlets for about six years. Perhaps a couple of generations of these owls must have enjoyed life in this hoary giant of a tree. It was here that I once saw two shy and elusive Common Palm Civets.

In some lower valleys and along numerous stream-beds, the evergreen Pongam Oil Tree is widespread. "The seeds of this tree are oily," explains Professor Almeida, "and since they are dispersed by water you will often see these trees growing along stream-beds." The oil from the seeds is used as fuel for generators and lubricant for simple machines. In mid-August, I come across scores of Pongam Oil Tree saplings along the streams. Dwarfed by the aged trees, this is a perfect image of the forest's continuity. But only a few of the many saplings will survive to see another season.

Towards the north of the park, along Bassein Creek, grows the only patch of mangrove and it is the forest's sole, visible link to the sea. Flocks of migratory, aquatic birds can often be seen near the creek. Little Tern, Black-headed Gull, various other gulls, herons and an occasional stork can be seen not far from the busy Ghodbunder Road that intermittently runs close to the creek and connects two of the country's busiest highways. Woodland species such as the Indian Grey Hornbill and Greater Racket-tailed Drongo can be heard and sometimes sighted along with wetland birds like the Grey Heron and Black-capped Kingfisher, a timeless fusion of two distinct worlds.

A small diversion from Ghodbunder Road leads to Chenna Creek which lies just outside the park. It is a popular weekend spot for many but sadly an increasingly favoured site for washing trucks. One winter morning, I saw two leopards frolicking here. Mobbed by crows, within moments, the ravishing cats disappeared into the vegetation. A resident of this area informed me that he once saw a leopard swim across Bassein Creek to the Nagla block, the northern part of the park. But the width of the creek made this seem improbable.

The Nagla block is a hilly terrain but the hills here are lower than those in the southern block, the highest point being 260 m above sea level. The trees in this region are fascinating. There are some giant trees, including some very large specimens of Haldu. A walk along the main trail in Nagla is exhilarating – Indian Scimitar Babblers and Puff-throated Babblers can be heard over the unending roar of automobiles on the bustling Mumbai-Ahmedabad highway. The north-eastern periphery of Nagla adjoins larger forest patches of the Thane district.

TOP: *The orange-yellow flowers of Ashoka can be seen between February and May.*

BOTTOM: *Tall trees dominate the Nagla block.*

In the central and northern parts of the park, some rocky hilltops have a cactus-sprinkled dry terrain. Several hills here are interconnected by narrow plateaus – open landscapes which, like much of the forest, display a distinct character in each season. Slippery, verdant and wet during the monsoon, these rocky uplands are dry and golden for the rest of the year. By mid-October, after the rains, when the grass transforms into myriad hues of gold, the black of the rocks is overwhelming. On a trek in early November, while traversing the rocks around Kanheri, I notice a few nightjars take wing as a Blacknaped Hare bolts. The backdrop of the sprawling city dominates the landscape. Over the years, I have observed the city's expansion with growing unease.

One morning, in early November, I accompany Major Madhav Mhaskar to the rocky expanse around Kanheri, now a golden-brown and black. An ex-army officer who studied geology, Major Mhaskar blends his subject with nature study quite admirably. "This rocky, hilly terrain forms an outer margin of the enormous Deccan Trap, the largest basalt plateau of the Upper Cretaceous-Eocene period between 136 and 65 million years ago," he informs. "A series of quiet volcanic eruptions created this plateau, the lava spreading slowly as horizontal beds that became interspersed with later intrusions in the form of sills and dykes," elucidates Major Mhaskar as he examines the rocks. "These basalts comprise minerals such as augite, calcite, chalcedony, magnetite, plagioclase, quartz and zeolite," elaborates the soft-spoken Major, who obviously finds considerable meaning and purpose in these gloomy rocks.

The largest rocky area lies immediately around and above Kanheri Caves. At its southern extremity, this imposing mass of rock drops abruptly into the valley, a sheer precipice of nearly 50 m. This is where I first saw the Shaheen Falcon plucking the feathers of a parakeet, in December 1973. Joslin and I observed it from a distance of 10 m, leaning precariously over a ledge, as did Humayun Abdulali on more than one occasion, ignoring the steep, slippery slope in his enthusiasm. I have seen the falcon here many times since then. These impeccable raptors often frequent this cliff that is a weekend rock-climbing site for six months of the year. Scores of enthusiasts learn this adventure sport that I tried once but soon gave up. The ledge of this rock offers a panoramic view of the lakes.

The two lakes, Tulsi and Vihar, continue to meet a part of Mumbai's immense water requirements and this is an important argument for increasing awareness about the forest and redoubling efforts to protect it. Created over 125 years ago to meet the city's water needs, these two impoundments are geographically located within the park but their waterspread areas are under the control of Mumbai's municipal corporation. Between them, the lakes account for just under eight percent of the park's area and continue to provide nearly five percent of the city's water needs. Over hundred million litres of water is drawn from these lakes every day.

The lakes and their margins are additional habitat types in the park. Our nature walks from the park's southern entrance often terminate at Vihar Lake, its open, grassy expanse attracting a lot of winter birds. Vihar Lake is the older and

TOP: *A superbly camouflaged gecko on a rock near Kanheri Caves.*

BOTTOM: *A sheer rock-face looming over the catchment forests of Tulsi Lake.*

larger of the two lakes, while Tulsi Lake, over a kilometre to the north and girdled by low, forested hills, is more scenic. The landscape around Tulsi Lake has its own charm and a walk along the 'tunnel trail' is an unforgettable experience. It can be quite unsettling in the late evening when the calm of the lake waters is punctuated by the loud, penetrating cries of a Red-wattled Lapwing and the musical notes of a Jungle Owlet, with muted sounds of people in the foliage-hidden forest guest house nearby. A leopard can often be seen wandering across the road . I have witnessed this remarkable scene no less than four times, in more or less the same way, almost as though it were a staged performance.

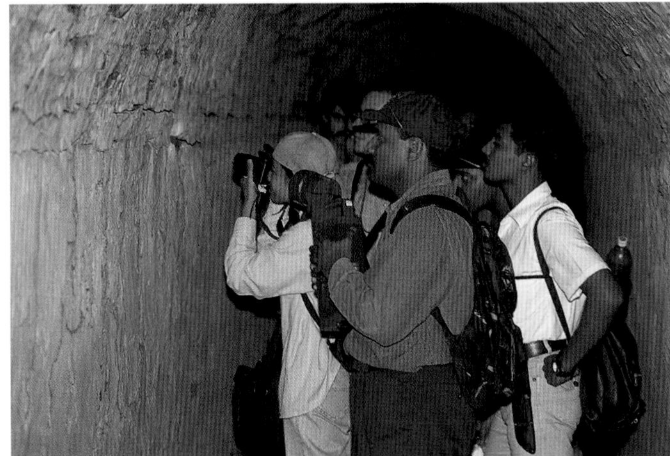

In marked contrast is the open expanse around Vihar Lake. This is an amphitheatre, a setting for continuous drama. From the grass cover, I observe a herd of forty Spotted Deer cautiously emerge from the surrounding forest and walk to the water, the stags lost in playful sparring; hear the eerie, quavering cry of the rare Mottled Wood Owl; see flocks of Lesser Whistling-duck overhead, their shrill whistles audible well before they've been sighted; hear the alarm calls of langurs in a distant hill, the guttural croak of a lone heron, the slithering of a Common Ratsnake. But the urban world is never out of sight and the massive form of the residential towers beyond Powai Lake can be seen from here.

There is plenty of bamboo in the forest. This wonder grass is more widespread in the central and northern parts of the park. The creaking sound of bamboo swaying in the tropical breeze, the mellow notes of a Indian Scimitar Babbler, the pleasing jingle of a Tickell's Blue Flycatcher and the cackle of a wary Red Spurfowl lends an indescribable charm to the forest. "There are two species of bamboo here," says Professor Almeida, "the Thorny Bamboo is more widespread than the Solid Bamboo." Among the many interesting characteristics of bamboo is its mass-flowering. "The Solid Bamboo blooms every forty years or so though sporadic flowering may be witnessed in some populations, while the Thorny Bamboo blooms perhaps once in a century," informs Professor Almeida. I have not come across anyone who recollects seeing the Thorny Bamboo in bloom here and have myself seen just a few specimens of the Solid Bamboo flowering in 1984.

Teak and bamboo are typical of a mixed-deciduous forest and lend a distinct character to it. Bamboo often dominates a landscape, usually at the expense of various herbs and shrubs. But an even more conspicuous flowering plant is the Karvi shrub. It is ubiquitous and forms the dominant ground flora over large tracts of the park. For much of the year there are endless rows of dry stalks, used by the local people for building the walls of their homes. Early in the monsoon, Karvi forms a green carpet as fresh foliage erupts low over the ground. Within a few weeks it resembles a tall barrier, perhaps the most striking change in the forest landscape – a thick curtain of foliage concealing much of the drama of life in the park.

TOP: *Searching for lizards and spiders in the contour trench near Tulsi Lake.*

BOTTOM: *Towering apartments are visible from the sprawling expanse around Vihar Lake.*

The Sanjay Gandhi National Park is just minutes away from the congested and polluted city of Mumbai. The view of glass, concrete and steel from some areas in the park (above) is a grim reminder of the proximity of the urban world to this forest.

Much of the park's terrain is hilly. These hills form the outer spur of the Western Ghats – a biodiversity hotspot. Dominating the park's landscape, along its eastern and western edges (above right), is a peripheral range of hills generally running north to south, interspersed with shorter offshoots. Beginning from near sea level, the landscape reaches a height of 486 m (right) northeast of Kanheri Caves.

The view from the cactus-strewn, rocky upland above Kanheri Caves is of an extensive valley (above). The two lakes, Tulsi Lake in the foreground and Vihar Lake at some distance, appear amid a bowl-shaped sprawl of mixed-deciduous forest. The vegetation between the lakes comprises original forest and secondary growth. The park's paved main road, skirting the lakes, cuts through this landscape.

The area around Kanheri Caves is essentially composed of basalt rock, interspersed with ash beds. In the vicinity of the caves, extensive tracts of dark, exposed rocks (left) sporadically encrusted with grass and cacti, vividly contrast with the surrounding forested hills. Towards the southern margin of the rocky stretch above the caves is a precipitous cliff, popular with weekend rock-climbers and a pair of Shaheen Falcons.

The park is divided into two unequal parts – the southern block is more extensive while the northern Nagla block extends over just 16 sq km. The Nagla block is characterised by tall forest with towering specimens of Haldu trees. This forest can be seen in the low-lying tract along the main trail leading east from the highway, past the small village of Sasupada that is home to several tribal families. A fallen tree creates a clearing (above) that shows signs of invasion by a host of opportunists, making the most of such sunlit gaps. Fallen wood replenishes the soil and serves as a greenhouse for saplings. Age-old agricultural practices are still followed around the park. A few families cultivate paddy (rice) in clearings (top) during the monsoon, their crops frequently attracting wild boar, domestic livestock and pariah-dogs – tempting prey for leopards. This inevitable contact between people and nature is the most critical development in the recent history of this troubled but unique wilderness.

Running through the park, Bassein Creek (above left) forms its natural divide, creating the two blocks. The northern hills are lower and less precipitous than those in the southern areas. Korlai Hill, the highest point in the Nagla block, is nearly 260 m above sea level. The north-eastern periphery of this part of the park is almost contiguous with the larger forested tracts of the adjoining Thane district. Where forest meets sea water in an estuary (left), the view is archetypically tropical. A narrow belt of mangrove forest forms the foreground. Distinctively demarcated areas of different species are visible, clearly fashioned by their tolerance to salty water and the extent of silt-laden freshwater available. Eight species of mangroves have been identified in this two-kilometre-long stretch of the creek. Rising beyond the mangroves, to the north and south of the creek, is deciduous forest.

With the dramatic increase in road traffic over the past few years, the bridge over Bassein Creek (above) is unable to cope with the unending streams of automobiles on the Mumbai-Ahmedabad highway – one of the country's busiest roads. Construction of a wider bridge proceeds at a frantic pace. The forested tracts of the park's Nagla block intermittently touch National Highway No. 8.

Tulsi Lake, built in 1874, was created to supplement the larger Vihar Lake. Along the far end of the main dam lies a contour trench (above right), a water harvesting strategy. It is built along the curves of the hills to collect water from the surrounding slopes, increasing the lake's catchment area. Nearly two metres deep and almost as wide, this trench leads north from the lake towards Kanheri Hill. A walk through this trench, popularly referred to as the 'tunnel trail' by local nature enthusiasts, offers a unique eye-level view (right) of the forest floor.

The dominant vegetation type of this forest is mixed-deciduous (South Indian Moist Deciduous Forest), characterised by a majority of trees shedding leaves during the dry months (above), between mid-November and early June. There are almost 800 species of flowering plants here, from lowly herbs to lofty trees. The Haldu is one of the tallest trees observed in the park today. A number of trees not indigenous to the region have come to dominate the landscape, at times depleting the original vegetation in several areas of the park.

The Karaya thrives on hard, exposed and rocky areas where the soil is shallow and most forest trees cannot take hold. Its pale grey-green bark, often almost white, invariably peels off in slender, papery plates, lending a peculiar charm to this tree (right) popularly known as the 'ghost of the forest'. The Karaya is striking, more so on a full moon night or when visible through the foliage of other forest trees. During December and January, when the tree is leafless, foul-smelling yellow flowers appear in bunches at the end of its branches (far right). It was on the leathery, maroon-red fruit of the Karaya that the Malabar Pied Hornbill and Great Hornbill, sighted in the park during February 2000, were observed feeding.

The carpet of dead leaves, twigs, fruits, animal remains and other organic matter is both nature's nursery and burial ground. This crackling, tawny spread of litter (above) covers the precious soil which sustains life and is also home to decomposers and scavengers. It is the fundamental law of nature that life is intricately bound with death and nothing can exist without the all-important soil.

The loss of leaves is a water conservation tactic typical to the deciduous forest. Leaf-fall (left) can begin in the very first month of the dry season, and for much of the period between end November and May the forest appears devoid of life. The leafless canopy, however, proves to be an asset. Leaves are profuse with water, even wasteful, as their surfaces release considerable amounts of this vital liquid through the process of transpiration. The leaf-fall thus ensures greater preservation of water and other nutrients in roots, stems and branches. The plants that have developed this important restorative mechanism are known as 'deciduous', derived from the Latin word *decidere* which means to 'fall off'.

Water is essential to all life on earth, be it in the Amazon rainforest or in Mumbai's national park. The shortfall or abundance of this elixir of life brings about the most dramatic changes in the landscape of the park. The forest's response to this inorganic, chemical compound is almost illusory. Water will be the crucial factor determining the future of this forest, and of every other surviving wilderness. Featured here (above, left and following pages) are a series of before-and-after habitat images photographed in the arid summer months and again during the monsoon.

The two man-made lakes, Tulsi Lake and Vihar Lake, are a highlight of this park. Tulsi Lake (above) is girdled by low hills with dense forest cover. On a hillock overlooking the eastern periphery of this lake lie the masonry ruins of an old rest-house, built during its construction, more than 125 years ago. This setting offers a magical view of the lake and its surroundings.

Spread over 7.26 sq km, Vihar Lake (right) was created in 1860 by damming the valley of the Gopar river. The construction of the dams and the laying of pipelines cost 37,36,500 rupees, a substantial sum at that time. Delivery of water from this lake to the city began in 1860. By 1881, Vihar Lake supplied a little over forty-five litres of water per person per day. Today, it supplies ninety million litres per day which is nearly four percent of Mumbai's immense water supply. The effective catchment area of this lake, in the southernmost expanse of the park, spreads over 18.96 sq km. The vast, grassy sprawl around its northern and western margins is a haven for wildlife, particularly winter-visiting birds.

BWW

The inward slopes of the park's peripheral mountains along with their offshoots constitute the catchment area of Tulsi Lake. The dam, located on the western end of the lake, is visible at the bottom centre of this aerial view (above) of the lake's catchment forests. Densely forested, this terrain has remained relatively undisturbed for over a century.

With a waterspread of 1.35 sq km, Tulsi Lake (above left) cost a mere 4,50,000 rupees to build. It was originally planned that water from Tulsi Lake would be drained into the adjacent Vihar Lake whenever required. In 1877, at a further cost of 33,00,000 rupees, a massive project was launched to transport water through an extensive pipeline (left) from Tulsi Lake to the top of Malabar Hill in south Mumbai.

A full moon rises over the waters of Tulsi Lake (above) – such simple splendour can entrance even the most uninitiated. In the wild, behind the deceptive quiet of the night, the battle for survival carries on unnoticed.

A pre-dawn glow lights up the sky beyond the hills girdling Tulsi Lake (left). The transition from night to the gentle radiance of dawn is a sequence of gradual, subtle changes. The Brown Fish Owl lets out a loud and eerie cry as the alarm calls of a Spotted Deer suggest the presence of a leopard nearby. The vigilant Grey Junglefowl clucks as an animal cry shatters the silence of the peaceful forest. These sounds are drowned by the roar of a passing aircraft – Mumbai's international airport is barely ten kilometres to the south of this fragile setting.

A stream, off the Silonda trail, overflows with rainwater (above). During the monsoon, the park receives nearly 250 cm of rain in less than four months, transforming its landscape dramatically. An assortment of seemingly minor and insignificant streams typify this landscape and it is easy to forget that you are within the limits of a giant metropolis. Sometimes as wide as 50-70 m, the longest stream extends to nearly eight kilometres. This intricate network of brooks, torrents and gushing waterfalls forms the framework for the forest's functioning. Water transpired by the trees returns as rain and in a timeless cycle accumulates as precious groundwater, crucial to all life in the forest.

Growing along the park's numerous streams, the Pongam Oil Tree is a widespread evergreen tree. Flowing water carries its oily seeds. Some get trapped amid pebbles, in cracks in the soil and in the tangle of older roots where they quickly germinate. By mid-monsoon, innumerable saplings sprout along the watercourses, dwarfed by older trees, as seen (right) along a brook near the Silonda trail.

While large trees – the pillars that constitute the forest's fundamental design – may be its most impressive component, they are outnumbered by species of smaller plants (above). For every plant, from leafless fungi to herbs, bamboos and smaller trees, survival is a constant struggle – obtaining adequate sunlight, nutrients and water to survive. The forest is a highly organised, complex manufactory that is also extremely energy-efficient and in some subtle and not-so-subtle ways the great trees seem to provide ample support to the smaller herbs, climbers and epiphytes.

A forest is like an energy bank (right). Green plants have the unique ability to absorb solar energy and they use it to convert water, carbon dioxide and minerals into vital oxygen and powerful organic compounds. This trapped energy is stored in the form of foliage and wood, and all animal life depends upon the organic beneficence of the forest.

LIFE IN THE

CITY FOREST

The forest is thrilling at all times. There is never a dull moment as it is teeming with myriad forms of life. The two hours after daybreak are a time of bustling activity aroused by the sun. A few hours in the morning sunshine and I feel at peace with the world around me. My senses are heightened and I can see the beads of dew slowly evaporate from every blade of grass.

On a Sunday morning in early October, my wife, Jyoti and I leave home at 6:20 and are joined by a few friends. Within twenty minutes we are in the forest near the park's southern entrance at Goregaon. At 6:55, we catch a glimpse of a leopard ambling across the road near the Conservation Education Centre of the Bombay Natural History Society (BNHS). It slides down the slope and vanishes in a flash. "You could call it the centre's resident cat; it spends many days in a drainage culvert," says Deepak Apte, Education Officer at the centre. Common Langurs keep up their garrulous alarm calls for the next five minutes until they can no longer sense the spotted cat's presence. Within an hour of leaving home we have already encountered, besides the leopard and the langur troop, several species of birds – Grey Junglefowl, Red Spurfowl, Greater Racket-tailed Drongo, Indian Grey Hornbill, Emerald Dove, Black-hooded Oriole, Puff-throated Babbler and White-eyed Buzzard.

We reach a quarry, a disused depression close to the southern entrance of the park that becomes a tiny pond of life for half the year. A Barking Deer can be heard intermittently for the next half hour from a nearby hill. A Green Sandpiper– one of the earliest winter migrants in the park – is disturbed by our presence and takes off, screaming agitatedly. A Little Cormorant circles overhead before flying off, perhaps to Vihar Lake. By November, the water-level of the pond will recede and signs of numerous animals and birds at its edge will be visible. We proceed towards Pongam Valley and – encountering Owl Moths, Stick Insects and mantis on the way – add over twenty species to our bird list.

An Owl Moth resting on a damp rock-face.

An hour and a half later, on the margins of the flooded Vihar Lake we encounter a Grey-breasted Prinia family, the adults busy feeding their three fledglings. A flock of Little Cormorants basks on bush-tops, their wings outstretched and glistening, as a pair of Whiskered Terns gambol in low flight. An Indian Bull Frog makes an enormous leap as grasshoppers spring about the green but wilting grass. Walking back towards the tree cover, I run into an enormous web of a Giant Wood Spider, its fine, silken strands getting entangled in my beard. Within minutes the female spider has repaired her web.

The park's web of life seems as intricate and self-restoring as the spider's. I have often marvelled at the large variety of life forms in the park which lies in one of the world's most congested and polluted cities. One of the reasons for the park's amazing biodiversity is its location. Not very far from the Western Ghats, the forest lies at the tip of a biologically rich region that experiences heavy rainfall. It receives about 250 cm of rain in just over three months and there is enough warmth to sustain all forms of life. The varied topography within and around the park explains nature's largesse.

The monsoon is over and October marks the beginning of one more cycle of seasons, of the forest's return to simplicity and stringency after a period of extravagance and grandeur. It is quite warm and humid. Under the azure sky, often tempered with fluffy cumulus and delicate cirrus clouds, brilliantly coloured butterflies flash by. There are over 150 species here, more than twice as many as have been located in Great Britain.

The second half of the monsoon, early August to mid-September, is the best time for locating insects, especially caterpillars. There are all kinds of these leaf-munchers, from hairy giants to loopers and myriad cloak-and-dagger maestros resembling twigs, leaves and bird-droppings, a few measuring an incredible 10 cm in length. "The last few weeks of rain, the increasing heat

of the sun, luxuriant herbage, humidity, an abundance of food plants – these are perfect conditions for butterflies to multiply," enthuses Naresh Chaturvedi, Curator of the BNHS, an entomologist with a passion for butterflies. They have been mating and multiplying all through July and August and in the six weeks following mid-September they will virtually explode into view.

During this period, I have sometimes located over thirty species of butterflies in a day. From the dwarfish Tiny Grass Blue, less than two centimetres in length, to the whopping Blue Mormon, with a wing-span of 15 cm, butterflies typify life at its joyous best. Nocturnal moths are more diverse than butterflies but it is not very clear as to how many species exist. V Shubhalaxmi, Education Officer at the Conservation Education Centre, has been documenting moths for several years. "I have so far collected over fifty species," she says, "and though my study is narrow-based with special emphasis on Wild Silk Moths and Hawk Moths, I must admit that even at a most conservative estimate there would be at least four times as many species of moths here as there are of butterflies." One evening in late September, my friend, Sanal Nair and I encountered thirty-two kinds of moths around the Log Hut, the forest rest-house overlooking Tulsi Lake.

Among the insects in the park are quick-change artists – masters of camouflage and disguise. There are poisonous insects, their jewel tones advertising danger and warning potential predators to keep off. Battalions of biting, bombarding bees, flies and wasps are a true test of endurance in the outdoors. Despite so much diversity and easy viewing, there is surprisingly little data on the variety of insects in the park. "To be honest," avers Chaturvedi, "we haven't properly documented the insect wealth of this forest. In my estimation, the total number of species could possibly be as many as 8,000 to 10,000. I have so far identified twenty species of ants, nineteen of mantis, and 150 or more of butterflies. We only have a vague idea of the variety of beetles, flies, grasshoppers, moths and other insects."

Close encounters with insects are relatively common in the park and this helps people, especially children, establish a bond with the natural world. The easy access to this forest offers them an opportunity to observe nature. When children hold a grasshopper or a glistening beetle or come face to face with an Owl Moth as big as 12 cm, there is a noticeable change in their perception of the so-called lowly insects. They rub their eyes in disbelief when they learn that a Harvester Ant's nest can store up to two kilograms of painstakingly collected grain or that the large 'eyes' on the wings of an Owl Moth are just a pattern.

TOP: *Moth caterpillars huddle on a leaf, deterring predators.*

CENTRE: *A lizard avoids a brightly coloured beetle which could be harmful to it.*

BOTTOM: *A colourful bug settles on its food plant.*

The Conservation Education Centre strives to create an awareness about the forest, and nature conservation through education is its primary mission. I accompany Prashant Mahajan, Senior Education Officer at the centre, and a group of children he is guiding through a nature trail. He draws the children's attention to the calls of a peafowl and the intricate web of a Giant Wood Spider. "Every week of the year," he tells me, "the centre organises interactive programmes for students, teachers, government officers, corporate and defence personnel with an aim to widen the support base for biodiversity conservation and to promote environment-friendly practices. We have a discovery room, a display room and an auditorium, and the nature walks are prefaced by theme-based in-house activities including films and slide-shows." For the past couple of years, the centre has been interacting with nearly 10,000 students and adults annually.

Repulsive though they may seem to most people, insects play an important role in the forest. These creepy-crawlies are the meek and the mighty. They have seen the dinosaurs come and go and have outlived the tiger in this park. They are among the greatest of architects and builders. Besides the termites that construct undulating, sometimes cliff-like edifices of mud, there are tiny Harvester Ants that create fortress-like nests with a central entrance and exit. Chaffs of grain strewn beside these remarkable homes are evidence of the activity of toiling busybodies that are smaller than a grain of rice.

The teeming multitudes of insects bring predators in their wake. If insects demonstrate awesome survival strategies, impartial nature ensures that predators do not lag behind. For every camouflaged, foul-smelling insect the forest has a predator to match. A mantis hunts its prey – usually some other insect – by ambush. It is in this park that I once saw a mantis showing off its colours, the only time I witnessed this unique display. There are fifteen kinds of lizards in the park and insects are all they are after. Most forest birds breed between May and July so that their young can feast on the profusion of insects during the monsoon. Mammals, from bats to rodents, would not survive were it not for insects. But the greatest of insect hunters are the silent and scheming spiders.

The park abounds with spiders in an incredible array of forms. Over seventy varieties have been located in the park and there are many more. The best time for observing spiders is between end July and mid-November. While it is the web-weavers or orb spiders that people are familiar with, there are many that do not weave a web, preferring to hunt by ambush. The most widespread web-weaver is the Giant Wood Spider that emerges from its self-imposed hiding by early August, sometimes even sooner.

During one of my visits, I come face to face with a female Giant Wood Spider in her web. She is big, with a body nearly six centimetres long and eight legs radiating in all directions. Slung across a forest path, her web is huge, sometimes a metre in diameter or even bigger. I look for contact strands and supports. They are at least three metres long on either side. At times, the distance between the two furthest points on the web can be six metres. Occasionally, she makes her web high in forest

TOP: *A Bonnet Macaque leaps across to a higher branch.*

BOTTOM: *The protective colouration of the Indian Chameleon makes it difficult to detect.*

trees and sometimes even on the steel frames of transmission towers, but most of the time they are within three metres of the ground. When backlit, with droplets of water clinging to its strands, the web is a glorious sight. I count one occupied web per hundred metres along either side of the Silonda trail and the path to the park's highest point. Evidence, albeit circumstantial, of the tremendous diversity and abundance of insect life in the park.

The great insect extravaganza ends as suddenly as it begins. By early November, insects retreat, some transform into dull-coloured forms but the majority simply disappear with each passing day. With insects departing, spiders too begin to withdraw and by mid-November the first signs of dry weather set in. It is almost as if every living thing in the forest knows that the monsoon has ended. The complex chemistry of life in the park quickly responds to the extreme change in weather.

Most of the forest's smaller creatures have apparently finished their activity for the season. As eggs or larvae, pupae or adults, they find shelter in dark, protected corners, deep cracks in the earth, under flakes of bark or fallen logs and in cavities in rotting wood. Here they will lapse into aestivation, a phase of suspended animation. Some species still remain active, avoiding the heat of the day and emerging at night, and I spot some beetles, crickets and moths in the flashlight. Naresh Chaturvedi throws light on this interesting development, "There are several butterflies and grasshoppers, among other insects, that presumably face no shortfall of food and are prepared for the dry season. Several undergo a change in outward appearance to merge with the surroundings, a dry world of browns, yellows and russets."

The post-monsoon change in the park is quite rapid. A few weeks earlier visibility from the road was hindered by a curtain of Karvi growth and other floral profusion but now it is possible to see many metres into the forest. This marks the beginning of the finest bird-watching period in the park. Winter migrants from the Himalayas and beyond and a few local migrants from several hundred kilometres around the park, begin arriving by early September. Among the earliest bird to arrive is the Long-tailed Shrike. It mostly keeps to the scrub areas on the park's periphery but a pair or two can be seen around Vihar Lake. October sees an avian influx, with over a hundred species of winter visitors spreading over the many kinds of terrain in and around the forest. My bird tally for this park is 274 species.

Many forest birds are well into nesting by the onset of monsoon and much of the breeding is over by mid-August. However, the monsoon foliage hides the birds and it is in the period between December and March that they are most visible. At this time there are more leaves on the forest floor than on the trees and sightings are plenty. One balmy day in mid-January 1984, Joslin Rodrigues and I counted 123 species of birds, seen and heard over a seven-hour bird watch covering the area between the park's south gate at Goregaon and Kanheri Hill. Only during my trips to Bhutan and the famous bird sanctuary in Bharatpur have I bettered that record.

TOP: *With the advent of summer, the Short-horned Grasshopper turns a dull brown.*

BOTTOM: *A Black-naped Monarch builds its nest, bound on the outside with cobwebs and eggshells of spiders.*

Between January and May, the ground and cavity nesters breed. Grey Junglefowl and Red Spurfowl lay eggs amid dry leaf-litter and stones while a few woodpeckers display their carpentry skills. The Rufous Woodpecker digs its nesting cavity in the nests of some tree ants. In the summer of 1985, I found seven of its nests along the park's main road. Since the early 1990s the number of woodpeckers, like several other birds here, seems to be on the decline. There is a need for a comprehensive documentation of the park's avian diversity. I once saw twenty-three Indian Grey Hornbills fly overhead, one after another, into the forested Pongam Valley, and eleven on another occasion. In February 2000, my bird-watching colleagues and I encountered the Malabar Pied Hornbill and Great Hornbill, the first ever sightings of these huge birds in this part of the country. We often sight up to forty species in the short stretch of road along Pongam Valley, one of the finest bird-watching areas in the park.

While the forested areas and valleys are the haunts of barbets, leafbirds, cuckoo-shrikes, flycatchers, hornbills, minivets, sunbirds, woodpeckers and so many others, the lakes and their marshy edges have a distinct featherfolk. Around Vihar Lake, larks, pipits and a couple of Red-wattled Lapwings breed. In winter this sprawling open tract comes alive with bird activity.

Blue Rock Thrush, Common Stonechat, Black Redstart, Common Hoopoe, Bluethroat – Vihar Lake's precincts have a bird life all their own. Small bands of restless wagtails frolic by the waterside, frequented by Pheasant-tailed Jacana, Bronze-winged Jacana, Purple Swamphen, Little Cormorant, Grey Heron, Purple Heron and various egrets and sandpipers. Painted Storks, Asian Openbills and Black-headed Ibises can sometimes be seen feeding in deep waters. Each winter there is tremendous variation in the number of birds visiting the lake. Waterfowl come to the edge of the lake on winter mornings, their numbers fluctuating by the day. On some mornings there are hundreds of birds, a bevy of species. A few days later, hardly any can be seen. Perhaps the two lakes here are just fleeting stopovers for migrating waterfowl.

Predatory birds too frequent the lakes where I have seen more than ten species. An Oriental Honey-Buzzard flies overhead and the long-drawn, plaintive three-note whistle of a soaring Crested Serpent Eagle can be heard over a nearby hill. Black-shouldered Kite, Brahminy Kite, Black Kite, Eurasian Marsh Harrier and an occasional Grey-headed Fish Eagle fly low while White-bellied Sea Eagles and Booted Eagles soar high over the lakes. Bassein Creek attracts sea eagles and an occasional Osprey. The Shaheen Falcon flies overhead to its feeding site on the rock above Kanheri. One winter morning, I saw a Laggar Falcon darting over Vihar Lake, just missing a parakeet in flight. An Osprey pair spends much of the winter over the calm waters of Tulsi Lake and I often observe this majestic raptor hunt – a timeless performance.

Spotting birds is exhilarating but listening to them can give an even greater pleasure. To have Grey Junglefowl, Malabar Whistling Thrush and White-rumped Shama calling so close to my suburban home is exciting. After years of experience, I can rely on bird calls as well as their sightings to identify them. While nearly all ground and cavity nesters, including radiant kingfishers, are highly vocal, there is one species that deserves special mention – the Greater Racket-tailed Drongo. It is a veritable exhibitionist, a mimic nonpareil, often confounding bird-watchers into listing species not present. I have heard a drongo imitate calls of many birds, including the Crested Serpent Eagle and Shikra. It is a common bird here and without it this forest would have been markedly less captivating. The Greater Racket-tailed Drongo is one of the six species of drongos found in this forest. I doubt if as many varieties of drongos exist in any other city.

The restless Grey Wagtail searches for insects on the damp ground.

As the mild Mumbai winter fades into the rising heat of summer, there is a short burst of floral splendour. During the monsoon it is chiefly herbs and shrubs that bloom but the dry season ushers in a gregarious flowering of trees. In the months of January and February, the Red Silk Cotton tree is in bloom, its rich, pinkish-red vividly contrasting with the leafless canopy and an azure sky. I have observed twenty-six species of birds – drongos, babblers, leafbirds, bulbuls, minivets, ioras and flycatchers, besides the House Crow, Large-billed Crow and Common Myna – visiting these flowers. An occasional squirrel can be seen feeding on these flowers. Near Culvert No. 56, one of the many culverts in the park, the rocks are bordered with several Red Silk Cotton trees and on a good morning quite a few woodland birds can be sighted. It was here that I came across a riotous gang of nine belligerent Greater Racket-tailed Drongos, on a January morning.

It is early February and I am on the Yeur trail. A vivid orange cluster of flowers in the brown and pale green of the forest catches my eye. The Flame of the Forest looks spectacular and is a fortnight's bonanza for forest birds. The Indian Coral Tree has flowered too and its glowing scarlet flowers lasting nearly a month, are visited continuously by birds for nectar. April announces the flowering of the Indian Laburnum, its drooping flowers an exhilarating shade of lemon-yellow. The Bonfire Tree in bloom is a beaming scarlet. This mass-flowering during the dry months breaks the monotony of dull browns and tawny shades that so characterise the forest at this time of the year. By early May, when the summer sun is at its most oppressive, an entire hillside in the tourism zone turns a flaming scarlet as the exotic Flamboyant Flame Trees flower. It is the most breathtaking sight before the monsoon.

The park lies in a region that does not experience the dramatic colours of autumn – the glorious russets, oranges and yellows. However, during the short-lived spring or its equivalent, beginning in March and lasting for about three weeks, the new foliage of certain forest trees makes up for this lack of colour. The pinkish-crimson of the new leaves of Ceylon Oak is beautiful. These trees, backlit by the morning sun, rival the finest autumnal scenes in peninsular India. In a few days, the pink and red will turn into a vivid green; leaves loaded with chlorophyll to ensure that the marvel of life is sustained.

During summer, the forest floor is a veritable carpet of dry leaves. Even my most gentle step is tumultuous and the loud crackling alerts every creature within a 100-metre radius. But on this same brittle carpet of leaves and twigs, the leopard's sinuous movement rarely gives away its presence. While a Puff-throated Babbler hops delicately, I look up to see a naked canopy bereft of leaves, a tapestry of nearly bare branches against a cloudless sky. Contrary to widespread belief, this loss of leaves is no disadvantage. In fact, it is a survival strategy – an adaptation for conserving scarce moisture.

The carpet of dry and spiritless leaf-litter is a vital shield that retains moisture and protects the invaluable soil on which countless creatures thrive. Ants, beetles, centipedes, earthworms, frogs, lizards, scorpions, toads, all take refuge in this russet carpet while waiting for the rains. With each progressing week, from mid-March onwards, the debilitating heat

TOP: *A Bonfire Tree in bloom.*

BOTTOM: *A Plum-headed Parakeet feeds on the flowers of the Flame of the Forest.*

becomes worse. In the parched forest I can see a Barking Deer sprinting away where I could only hear its cry during the monsoon. An enormous Sambar stag glares at me before bolting with an ear-splitting alarm cry. The elusive Fourhorned Antelope pair, on their way to Tulsi Lake, stare momentarily only to turn around and run, blending into the arid landscape. Small herds of Spotted Deer, sometimes as many as forty animals, play hide-and-seek in the woods, momentarily emerging on a clearing or a forest road.

Over the past decade, the forest department in association with Mumbai's municipal corporation has been releasing small numbers of captive-bred ungulates (mostly Sambar and Spotted Deer) with a view to replenish their population. Apart from over two hundred deer, about a hundred monkeys and wild boar have been released. The existing number of wild herbivores in the park is small and sightings are few and far between. The rutting call of Spotted Deer echoing through Pongam Valley is a good omen, I tell myself. A troop of macaques feeds greedily as the booming calls of a group of langurs resound through the forest. They become fidgety and restless as I walk below.

There have been occasions when the calls of an uneasy langur troop have helped me catch a glimpse of a leopard, the park's arch-predator. Pug marks, fresh droppings, resting spots and an unmistakable feline odour also indicate the presence of a large spotted cat in the vicinity. Regarded by many naturalists as the most adaptable and elusive of India's large cats, the leopard in a place like Mumbai's national park, surrounded by a sea of humanity, has raised many troubling questions. I have had just over a hundred sightings and all, except three, have been post-1987.

As summer advances, sightings in the night become more frequent. I recall an evening in March 1992, when I accompanied Vishwas Walke, the former Deputy Conservator of Forests, on one of his inspections. The summer had not set in completely. Fires, caused by human carelessness, had ravaged sections of the forest following the Mahashivratri festival during which large crowds of people had invaded the park. As darkness enveloped the forest, Walke and I spotted two leopards, a lone civet and a jackal. The *oo...uk* of a Brown Hawk Owl broke the silence and we saw the faint silhouette of a Jungle Owlet flying low across a rocky terrain in the side-glare of the jeep's headlights. On the dry, open area around Vihar Lake, we could see about a score of deer eyes gleaming in the sweeping beam of the moving vehicle. We saw a wild boar charging across the forest track. In the distance the lights of the residential complexes across Powai Lake were visible. The roar of an aeroplane momentarily drowned the sounds of the wild and I was once again reminded of the proximity of the urban world.

By early March the cicadas' chorus begins. These camouflaged insects have no close second when it comes to sheer amplification and through the summer their noisy calls drown almost every other sound in the forest. Their screechy clamour continues well after the rains have set in, hundreds

TOP: *A young Russell's Viper in a defensive posture.*

BOTTOM: *Cicadas on a tree branch.*

often calling together. A single cicada leads the way, soon joined by others, resulting in a deafening chorus. As in the case of frogs and toads, this serves to bring the neighbourhood population of the species together. Through summer and till the first few weeks of the monsoon, males will sing and strut and the voiceless females will have the final say in choosing mates from the boisterous many.

The Oriental Magpie Robin commences its singing around the same time as the cicadas' chirping. In a forest not generously endowed with singing birds this bird is a saving grace. It is a fairly common bird, both in the park and the surrounding city, a classic example of a forest bird adapting to the urban world. It hops on the lawns in the park's tourism zone, waiting expectantly for the right moment to catch an earthworm or insect offguard.

It is late March. As I trudge along the dry bed of the Dahisar river, a rustling sound alerts me. The slightest movement on the dry carpet of leaves can be heard easily. In the dull tawny and sandy-coloured river-bed, amid leaves, stones and twigs, a bright orange-red streak catches my eye. It is a male Forest Calotes, one of the fifteen species of lizards found here. This courting male is attempting to lure two female lizards in the vicinity. He follows them around a tree and while one of the females springs onto a higher branch, the other descends to the stream-bed. The aroused male jumps after her and the couple vanish into the surrounding, dry bush.

The forest becomes a virtual tinder-box in early May. It is warm even before sunrise but thanks to a cool, westerly sea-breeze the Mumbai region is spared the dreadful heat experienced a few hundred kilometres to the north and east. Even at nine in the morning, the summer sun is strong. Bird activity subsides early. There are faint tinges of green on the droughty forest floor and some flowers too. What amazing plants these are – surviving, when all else is dry and shrivelled, when the very soil seems parched. In some mysterious manner, these plants seem to have found enough water, or perhaps, they require only a small amount. I wonder what enables them to survive and bloom in this summer heat.

Deer, langur, hare and the infrequent wild boar can be spotted occasionally and the signs of their presence are seen usually around water. In a landscape abounding in withered stalks, it is confounding what these animals live on. With another three weeks before the monsoon sets in, life goes on in the forest with birds and beasts keeping to the shaded areas and regularly moving towards water. Over the last few years the forest department has created several waterholes but many of these run dry. There is some water at Phanasache Pani, one of the waterholes below Kanheri, where Vijay Awsare and I come across fresh leopard pug marks and the diggings of Sambar and wild boar. A wailing cry draws our attention to an Olivaceous Keelback snake that has caught a hapless frog. Spot Swordtail and Common Blue Bottle butterflies frequent the damp surroundings adding colour to the muted landscape.

One morning in late May, I sight a Pied Cuckoo, considered to be the harbinger of monsoon. With unfailing regularity it first appears between May 23 and June 4 every year. Accompanied by my bird-watching colleagues, Andrea Britto and Manisha Shah, I follow the bird-calls and locate four species of cuckoos, including the Banded Bay Cuckoo, Common Hawk Cuckoo and Grey-bellied Cuckoo. A peacock's loud call can be heard. On the park's outskirts,

A male Forest Calotes adds colour to the dull, summer landscape.

I hear the wheezing notes of the male Baya Weaver. The monsoon is now imminent. I know from past experience that the first rain will fall in the first half of June. It always does.

The monsoon breaks. An onslaught of howling winds, thunder and lightning, India's southwest monsoon is an immense flourish of nature's power. For days before the actual onset the weather remains unpredictable with passing showers, shadowy clouds and bracing intermittent winds. For the first few days the intense heat dissipates all efforts of the blackening clouds. Then, one day, the first showers arrive cutting through the heat. Nothing is more eagerly awaited though the rains are damaging for some. The world of certain summer-time spiders turns topsy-turvy as the downpour pounds their fragile webs into the dry grass. The first rains take the breeding ground-birds, numerous rodents and reptiles completely by surprise.

The rains result in wild magic and the deciduous Indian forest is a fine place to observe the monsoon's staggering effect. It is a tremendous generative force, animating the teeming life in the soil. It restores greenery to a dehydrated landscape, creating a luxuriance of emerald foliage. Even the lifeless pebbles on the park's numerous stream-beds shimmer and gleam in the rain.

As the earliest showers are sucked in by the parched soil, a heavenly fragrance arises from the earth. Frogs and toads emerge from hiding, their chorus of croaks a truly monsoonal sound. "Nine species of these amphibians exist here," says Isaac Kehimkar, a naturalist and Public Relations Officer at the BNHS. Indian Bull Frogs may reach an amazing 18 cm length while Ornate Narrow-mouthed Frogs are a mere two centimetres. Through the mist on the Jambulmal summit, I see a Short-headed Burrowing Frog on the forest floor. The Fungoid Frog is charming and I see some frogs resting on the floating pads of Water Lettuce. One rainy morning, I encounter a Fungoid Frog resting on the head of a buoyant Indian Bull Frog. "Tragically, over the last five years, amphibian population, here and elsewhere, have been declining," says Kehimkar. Groups of toads are certainly a thing of the past.

With the first showers emerges something else and in greater numbers than the amphibians. I look through my binoculars and observe crows, drongos and kites flying low over the forest across Tulsi Lake with no discernible purpose. I proceed towards the mass of birds and it seems they are after insects. A closer look reveals hordes of termites in the air and on the ground. Mobs of termites emerge from tiny holes in the ground, rustling and whooshing in a frenzy, some attempting to crawl clumsily up the grass stalks, low bushes and small rocks nearby. A lizard arrives at the entrance of a cavity to feast on these termites. There is a continuous outpouring – they are establishing a new colony.

The heavens darken to signal a downpour. Soon, the forest is filled with the fragrance of ecstatic, revived life. The listless, leafy carpet begins to drip with water. Glorious Pink-striped Trumpet Lilies sprout as if by magic but they barely last the first week of rain. While the background is still stark and unadorned, the lilies blossom as suddenly as they vanish. Wondrously coloured insects are everywhere, especially the ravishing Red Silk Cotton Bugs that feast on fallen fruits. All of blistering May, gangs of these foul-smelling bugs took shelter behind the flaky barks of the Karaya tree.

Red Velvet Mites can be seen crawling on the sodden soil along with numerous beetles and scorpions that have emerged from their summer retreats. Countless worms, bugs and flies can be observed crawling, feeding and mating. A mother Wolf Spider scuttles amid the sodden leaves below Kanheri Hill, carrying her swarming brood of young on her back. It is an astonishing sight. Within a week of extreme weather change she has emerged from hiding and has reproduced. Not very far

Lush green foliage covers the forest floor in the monsoon.

from this spider, a female scorpion hides in the cracks of a tree trunk with seven baby scorpions huddled on her back.

The monsoon brings with it a riot of colour, breaking the monotony of green. Beginning with a few scattered buds, within a few weeks forest clearings and roadside stretches are a colourful revelry of flowers. One of the most abundant shrubs is Karvi that mass-flowers after every seven years. When thousands of flowers bloom simultaneously it is a purple feast for the eyes. Throng of insects, from dazzling butterflies and secretive moths, to easygoing beetles and bugs, glut themselves on these flowers. Slothful snails too gorge on Karvi buds and flowers. While Karvi blooms every eighth year, there is a variety of other flowers that flourish every monsoon.

The Pink-striped Trumpet Lilies are the first to emerge and disappear, followed by the gorgeous pink and white flowers of the Hill Turmeric. For the next four months, I come across several flowering species. Malabar Glory Lilies, Garden Balsams, Sensitive Smithias, Sesame, Commelina and Costus are only some of them. In late September, several orchids burst forth on high plateaus. Over the years I've noticed a gradual change in species composition. Where there would usually be a pageant of Garden Balsam and Sensitive Smithia, Silver-spiked Cockscomb or Sesame have taken over. But succession is part of nature's design.

The rains inspire birds into frenetic activity. I had seen my first wild peafowl in the park, dancing in the rain, more than thirty years ago. "To see a peacock dancing before I reach my humdrum office is an ecstatic feeling, something I cannot do justice to in words," gushes a resident of the nearby suburb of Borivli. Among the many birds which are most prominent during the rains are the resident warblers. The Ashy Prinia, a semi-urban bird that is equally at home in city gardens and in scrubby areas at the edge of the forest, acquires a more colourful plumage. The Grey-breasted Prinia is the most conspicuous species during the rains and is also the most social.

Between May and July is the breeding season of drongos, orioles, bulbuls and many other birds, more or less coinciding with the arrival of the monsoon. The rains continue right through early September. I encounter restless fledglings, excitedly following their parents, clamouring to be fed. Sometimes, Joslin Rodrigues and I come across young birds that have fallen from their nests and his cottage becomes a sanctuary for these orphans. Over the last fifteen years, we have saved and released several bird species, including Black-hooded Oriole, Golden-fronted Leafbird and even the Grey Junglefowl.

It is early October and I am on the waterlogged margin of Vihar Lake. At the edge of the lake a Grey-breasted Prinia pair calls excitedly. Flocks of Little Cormorants bask in salubrious sunlight as a small band of terns dances in the air. Webs of countless spiders glisten as seed-rich reeds sway in the breeze. Small clouds of red, yellow and blue dragonflies rise above the verdant kingdom. Another year passes by and life carries on in the city forest.

TOP: *Large Costus flowers bloom by early August.*

BOTTOM: *The pod of a Milkweed plant bursts open, scatterimg its seeds.*

During the few weeks of spring beginning in March, the Ceylon Oak, a fairly common tree in the park, is a profusion of colours (above). Its new leaves start appearing by end February and for a short period these trees manifest numerous shades of crimson and deep pink. Gradually, with the development of chlorophyll pigments, the leaves begin to turn green.

Nature's colours have an important role to play in the eternal struggle for survival. Every suffusion of colour, be it a blurry streak or a distinct patch, serves a purpose for predator and prey alike. For the chameleon (top right), the grasshopper (centre right), the moth caterpillar (right), as for all life in the forest, these are the colours of existence.

In any forest, it is the towering trees that enthral and most people scarcely notice the forest floor. Yet, this vast spread of soil and leaf-litter is vital to the survival of life in the forest. Fungi silently perform the task of breaking down and decomposing organic matter (above). Red Silk Cotton Bugs attack a fallen fruit (top left). A skink lies hidden in the fertile carpet (centre left), waiting for unwary insects to come within striking distance. The chameleon, a terrific hunter, has fallen prey to a predator (left) – perhaps a bird of prey or a snake – and is returned as nutrient to the forest floor.

Denizens of the forest form remarkable alliances in search of food, light, shelter and transport. The struggle to obtain adequate sunlight is best demonstrated by the Strangler Fig (above). Germinating high in a tree, the tiny seedling develops two types of roots, one holding onto the host tree and the other growing towards the soil. The latter root quickens the development of the plant, supplying abundant nutrients and providing a labyrinth of supplementary roots that ultimately encase the supporting tree. At the base of Karvi stalks, on the park's highest point, the striking white and yellow flowers of a root parasite bloom at the height of the monsoon (top right). This little-known species is endemic to Mumbai and parts of the Western Ghats. Some parasitic plants can actually photosynthesise on their own, thereby ensuring their host's survival. The greatest association here is undeniably between birds and flowers, with nearly forty species of birds performing one of nature's greatest tasks – pollination. The Purple Sunbird (centre right) is an important flower-pollinating bird in the park. Tiny, colourful mites hold fast to a Short-horned Grasshopper, hitchhiking between different food sources (right).

When the summer sun is most oppressive and the park's landscape bone-dry, the Indian Laburnum blooms a cheerful shade of lemon-yellow. The flowers appear in clusters of drooping sprays (above) and peak flowering occurs between mid-April and early June. The long pods appear later in the year and are relished by monkeys who help in scattering its seeds. Wild boar feed on the pods strewn on the forest floor. The tall, buttressed Red Silk Cotton is a prominent tree in the park. Its stems and branches are encrusted with hard, conical prickles that may gradually disappear as the tree ages. Leaf-fall commences around early December and the crimson flowers (top), seen between late December and early March, are regularly visited by woodland birds. The finest cluster of these trees grows along an open, rocky site flanking the road between Tulsi Lake and Kanheri Caves.

Very early in the year, the Flame of the Forest begins to shed leaves. It takes a few leisurely weeks for this tree to transform into a flaming orange-red (left). Clusters of these trees seen during this period give an impression of a forest on fire. This medium-sized, deciduous tree is quite widespread throughout the park. When in bloom, many woodland birds visit its flowers (far left) for nectar. The ground below the tree is strewn with hundreds of flowers lending colour to the drab forest floor. Sometimes isolated trees bloom as early as end December.

Karvi carpets much of the park's landscape, from the lowest elevation to the highest point. The most conspicuous shrub of the forest, it looks just as marvellous during the dry months as in the monsoon. Fresh Karvi growth rises magically amid the towering, dry stalks of the previous season (above). This abundant shrub flowers every eight years. The buds appear by mid-July of the flowering year and the purple pageantry (top and centre left), sprinkled intermittently with a few bright pink flowers (left), lasts for nearly eight to ten weeks. The flowering of this shrub is a windfall for multitudes of insects that gorge on the plentiful petals and protein-rich nectar.

The Sensitive Smithia is a prolific monsoon herb growing close to the soil and is seen along trails and forest clearings in the lower reaches and on hillsides. In August, the grass-green carpet is sprinkled with vivid yellow flowers (above). As insects go on a rampage for the following four weeks, there is plentiful prey for spiders and little lizards. The Malabar Glory Lily is an annual climber and is part of the immense floral flourish that begins by late July, when the monsoon rains have ushered in a verdant extravagance. The slender leaves of this climber have pointed tips that coil around surrounding vegetation like herbs and low trees. By early August, its glorious flowers (top) – a vibrant motley of crimson, orange and yellow – bloom and last for a month. This plant, especially its bulb, has various medicinal applications.

The Commelina herb can be seen along every trail and road in the park. Despite its profusion it often escapes notice, attracting attention only by its elegant flowers in variable shades of blue (left). The caterpillars of several moths feed on this herb.

Within a few hours of the monsoon's arrival there are numerous signs of renewed life in the forest as the torpid, leafy carpet appears to regain consciousness. Against a stark and unadorned backdrop, an imposing crowd of Pink-striped Trumpet Lilies dominated by large leaves, emerges almost overnight. The buds appear soon after (above). These flamboyant, white and pink flowers bask in full glory (top and left) for barely three or four days before drooping and fading away. In just over a week they disappear, swamped under the broadening spread of monsoon foliage.

Along the rocky, open expanse between Kanheri Caves and Tulsi Lake, countless flowers of Garden Balsam form a dense, vivid screen (above). This succulent herb is the food plant of several Hawk Moths.

The forest is a phenomenal storehouse of biodiversity, a gene-bank of the wild forms of numerous species crucial to our survival. The Hill Turmeric is a monsoon plant that grows in abundance in the park. Its large, showy flowers (right) are one of the most vivid displays of the wet season. A wild relation of a cultivated spice, this plant serves as food and offers refuge to many insects and other life forms.

Moss (above) invariably grow in areas where the air is still and heavy with moisture. Along with liverworts, they form a huge plant group known as bryophytes. Diminutive, green, moisture- and shade-loving, moss constitute the middle step in the evolutionary ladder, somewhere between algae and ferns, and flowering plants. They anchor themselves to a surface with their thread-like appendages, often forming dense carpets. In the stillness of the forest, on tree barks and rocks, two plants form a symbiotic association. Lichens (top) are a blend of highly modified fungi and certain single-celled algae. It is believed that while fungi furnish algae with a moist, sheltered niche to survive, they acquire nutrients from the algae. The finest spots for observing lichens lie above Kanheri Caves. Several kinds of babblers, flycatchers and thrushes liberally use moss and lichens for building their nests.

Dainty ferns (left) – survivors of ancient forests of seedless plants known as pteridophytes – along with clubmosses and horsetails were the earliest successful colonisers of land. Even though this forest is not a fern stronghold, several species of these unobtrusive and enchanting plants continue to survive, usually growing in shaded areas.

The floor of the forest is the foundation of life in the park and home to its most vital organisms. Fungi, the great decomposers, are the decisive link in the intricate web of life (above, top, above right and right). They derive nourishment from decaying matter and help in converting it into precious organic wealth. The most familiar and conspicuous fungi are the mushrooms. In Mumbai's national park, June to August are mushroom months, when numerous species, a veritable hodgepodge of form and colour, can be located. Like all fungi, mushrooms lack chlorophyll and procure nutrients from other plants, living either as parasites, or more commonly, as saprophytes that thrive on dead and decaying plants.

Though the end of the monsoon is the finest time for observing butterflies in the park, the vivid blue-green flashes of the Common Blue Bottle can often be seen at the height of stifling summer. Many of these gregarious insects can be observed on the damp soil around waterholes and stream-beds (above), where they indulge in mud-peddling, picking up vital mineral salts from the soil.

In the dark and deep forest a waif-like butterfly flutters past. The Blue Oakleaf (right) is a celebrated cloak-and-dagger artist. On closing its wings, this splendidly coloured insect looks like a dry leaf (above right), complete with veins and blotches. While small numbers may be seen during the dry months, it is between mid-July and October that this butterfly is most conspicuous.

The Great Eggfly is an imposing butterfly, often seen basking in the sun between August and late October. When it flashes its wings open, the shimmering blue, oval patches with their glistening white centre look striking (above). This is a noticeably territorial species and it can often be seen chasing other butterflies away from its feeding grounds.

Open areas and clearings within and around the forest are the haunts of the large and flashy Crimson Rose (right). This restless insect is visible all through the year. The adults show a distinct liking for lantana flowers on which they impatiently hover for nectar, hardly landing for more than a few seconds. Its caterpillars feed on fresh leaves of the Birthwort creeper and several other forest plants.

The park abounds with large moths. One such moth is the Tussar Silk Moth (above) that attains a wing-span of up to 15 cm. Its pale-cream cocoons can be located between May and October on the Indian Jujube – an important food plant for caterpillars – found in the forest and surrounding suburban areas. The occasional, simultaneous emergence of several moths is a spectacular sight.

The world's largest moth is found in this park, where its sightings have increased dramatically over the past few years. The Atlas Moth (above left) is a giant insect, with a wing-span reaching a staggering 28 cm. It prefers moist, dark areas and its caterpillar (left) shows a great variation in colour and has been observed feeding on as many as eleven species of plants in the forest. Like many large moths, adult Atlas Moths do not feed, their sole function being to mate and lay eggs. Their feathery antennae studded with an elaborate network of sensory cells are very sensitive, more so in the males as they can ferret out females at considerable distances, attracted by the pheromones released by them.

A whole host of insects advertise their presence in the forest by their spectacular warning colourations. At first sight, the Painted Handmaiden Moth can be mistaken for a bee or a wasp. Its bright orangish-yellow and black wings, along with the brilliant crimson and blazing blue on its body, serve as a warning for potential predators. The caterpillar of this small moth feeds on the leaves of the creeper, Morning Glory, besides some other forest plants. This mating pair (above) was sighted in early November, near Tulsi Lake.

The Hitler Bug (right) displays one of the most striking warning colourations. Appearing dangerous has its rewards – its garish colour and frontage warns predators to keep their distance. This bug can often be seen in broad daylight on leaves and twigs in the open areas of the park. It survives only on plant juices and is most active and visible between July and November.

It is said that the mantis is the king of all warrior insects. Wading through the dense Karvi growth, one monsoon morning, a flash of colour caught my eye. Closer scrutiny revealed an Orchid Mantis, its wings spread wide (above). I wondered about the possible reason for this display – perhaps the mantis was disturbed by our intrusion into its territory or maybe this was simply a threat display, an attempt to thwart the possibility of a predator attack. Female mantis are cannibalistic and research confirms that barely a quarter of male mantis survive mating. The male has to be extremely cautious when approaching a female and he has often been observed attempting to catch her unawares – almost jumping onto her back when she is not looking, belying the legendary mantis fame for bravery. But dispassionate nature has a motive behind every move. Mating is successful despite the consumption of the male, in fact, some experts believe that the female gains by killing and eating her mate – she derives nourishment for her developing ovaries and ensures the fertilisation of the eggs. This male was one of the fortunate ones – surviving forty minutes of mating (top).

The mantis is among the greatest hunters in the park. Its habit of raising its forelegs pressed together gives the impression that it is praying (left) while it is actually an effective position from which it lunges at prey, usually other insects. The park has more than nineteen species of mantis, encountered chiefly between June and November.

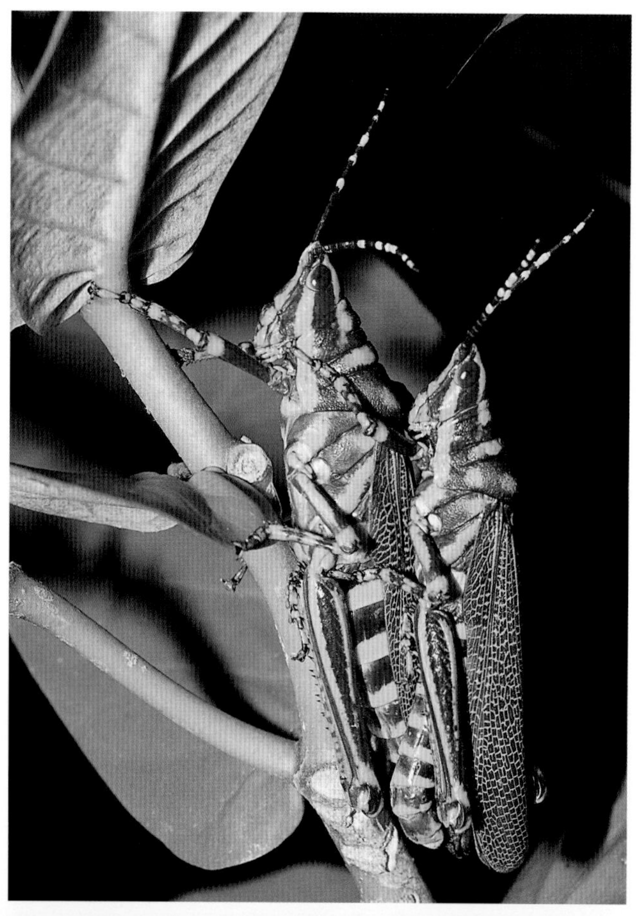

Enclosed within the insensitive covering of the exoskeleton, insects are not in immediate contact with their environment. But these six-legged creatures are recompensed for this deficiency by their antennae which come in astounding sizes. Highly responsive and sensitive appendages, antennae help insects feel the outside world, enabling them to smell, taste and decipher weather conditions. They enable insects to locate food and even help male moths find their mates. These finely tuned feelers have played a crucial role in the survival of insects. Some antennae can reach impressive dimensions – the feelers of this cricket (above) measure nearly 13 cm in length.

The Painted Grasshopper (above left) can sometimes be seen in the park's peripheral open tracts. One of the many insects that display warning colourations, it greedily devours the leaves of Milkweed, a poisonous plant seen along forest roads and in clearings, incorporating the poison in its own body. The Pied Cuckoo, a parasitic bird that is a monsoon-breeding visitor to this region, is one of the few predators observed feeding on this grasshopper, apparently impervious to its poison. On an overcast morning in early September, I observed a Short-horned Grasshopper (left) moulting on a Karvi stalk. Insects have a rigid, external skeleton that is cast off as they grow. The grasshopper's progress towards adulthood is marked by several moultings – its final transformation is into a winged form. It took this grasshopper nearly an hour to get rid of its old shell after which it remained clinging to the stalk for several hours. At first crinkled and pliable, its protective covering gradually gained in resilience.

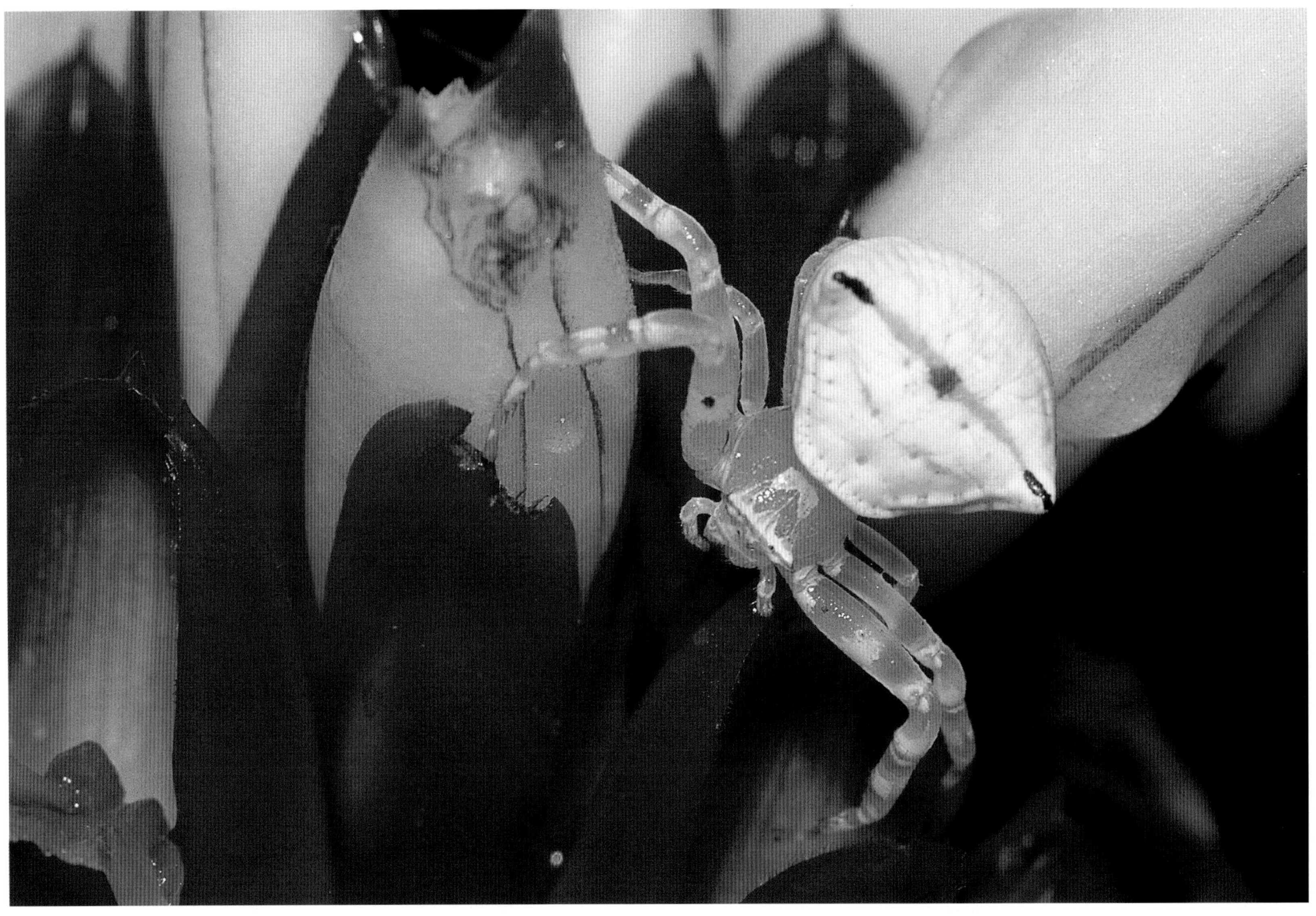

Once the monsoon rains have ushered in a floral profusion, the hunters emerge. On the petals of a Costus or Spiral Ginger flower, a Crab Spider (above), expertly camouflaged, waits for its prey. This roving spider does not weave a web but hunts by ambush, pouncing on and catching its prey in its jaws. Its short, strong legs help in tackling the trapped prey. It feeds on butterflies, bees and other insects that are attracted to the flower. This white variety of spider, quite widespread between August and late October, is not very easy to locate.

By mid- or late July, the first webs begin to appear (above right) and by mid-August they are everywhere. By all standards, the Giant Wood Spider rules the eight-legged realm of the park. The large spider commonly seen in the web is the female with a body nearly six centimetres long. The web she weaves is often a metre in diameter, slung across forest streams and paths. The contact strands and supports extending up to six metres, can sometimes be seen high up across forest trees but are usually within three metres from the ground. The fact this arachnid is so abundant here for over four months indicates that this is a flourishing wilderness. This spider's prey can include large insects like the Tussar Silk Moth (right).

Slow, silent snails are sometimes victims of assaults of sneaking glow-worms, a type of nocturnal beetle. The adults are usually luminous, many of a species often synchronising their lights to flash in a spectacular concert. The female of several glow-worms look like the larvae of some butterflies and moths. But unlike the larvae, she is not a vegetarian. She slowly advances towards her quarry, typically a small snail, and sets about eating into the sluggish mollusc (above). The snail's efforts at defensive frothing prove futile as the female glow-worm locks onto its succulent flesh.

A female Wolf Spider scampers through leaf-litter soggy with the first monsoon rains, a swarm of spiderlings clinging to her back (left), some falling off along the way. The female of several species of Wolf Spider is known to carry her brood of up to a hundred or more spiderlings for several days before the young disperse. This hunting spider relies on camouflage and surprise to hunt its insect prey.

In the leafy canopy of the forest, the Golden-fronted Leafbird remains largely unseen. Active and tetchy, it is an accomplished mimic. Besides its own repertoire of calls, it can imitate the calls of various forest birds, including drongos and the Shikra. While the bird's diet consists largely of insects, small berries and fruits, it regularly visits many flowering trees, like the Wild Guava, for nectar (above).

The Greater Racket-tailed Drongo (left) is a noisy bird, its shrill calls overshadowing other bird calls in the forest. Though insectivorous, it adores bamboo forests and visits flowering trees, especially the Red Silk Cotton, to feast on nectar. It is most belligerent during its breeding season from May to August – screaming and whistling like no other bird in the forest – when various birds of a meeker disposition take advantage of this vigilant 'security guard' by building their nests in and around the drongos' nesting trees.

Of the four species of sunbirds in the park, the male of the Crimson Sunbird (above) is breathtakingly beautiful – a psychedelic blend of bright crimson, metallic green, purple and bright yellow. It is a restless occupant of the middle and upper strata of the forest. More often than not it attracts attention by its sharp and distinctive calling.

Among the many birds conspicuous during the monsoon are several warblers. Of the three species of leaf-stitching warblers that seem to have divided the park between themselves, the Common Tailorbird is the one that usually keeps to urban areas. Though small numbers may be encountered in the forest, it is more prevalent in the peripheral tracts, nesting in wild-growing, large-leaved monsoon vegetation and amid cultivated garden plants and trees. Here (left), a male is seen approaching his nest in the park's tourism zone.

The Indian Grey Hornbill is a large, boisterous bird that is frequently sighted and heard in the park. It breeds between February and June and has a peculiar nesting strategy. After mating, the female seals herself in a tree-cavity, the male assisting her from outside. She remains enclosed all through incubation and until a few days after the eggs have hatched, fed by the male through a narrow opening in the cavity (above). She then joins her tired mate in feeding their insatiable young for the following four to six weeks.

The Rufous Woodpecker is the only bird in the forest seen cohabiting with insects during nesting. It chisels a cavity in the football-sized nest of certain tree ants. The bird begins carving into the nest by late February, taking a week to create a hollow large enough for it to settle in (right). The young are reared while this nest is teeming with its original inhabitants. Exactly how the ants benefit from the association is not clear but this is one of the many relationships that enliven the seemingly monotonous summer.

A bevy of aquatic birds, both residents and winter visitors, frequent the mangroves along Bassein Creek and the marshy margins of Vihar Lake. Small flocks of Brahminy Kite (above) are regularly seen over the creek where the White-bellied Sea Eagle and Osprey also hunt. On some winter days, numerous gulls and egrets appear at the mouth of the creek (top), feeding frantically on a wealth of organic detritus. The largely crepuscular Little Heron is a secretive marsh bird, occasionally appearing in open areas along the creek. Here (above left), a heron has been caught by a tribal boy at the edge of the park's Nagla block. The elusive Slaty-breasted Rail keeps to the creek (left), seldom frequenting the lake.

The Oriental Magpie Robin (above) is a member of the rich-voiced thrush family and its joyful singing has a clarity of tone. Its apparently random and loud, unclouded carolling is remarkable. Silent and unobtrusive during the later half of the monsoon and all through winter, this bird's singing begins by early March. It can usually be heard in the early mornings but may pour forth snatches of song intermittently through the day. It moves with equal ease on lawns and dappled forest floor, regularly visiting trees laden with fruits and flowers.

Rummaging for insects on the forest floor, amid fallen leaves and damp litter, the Puff-throated Babbler (left) is a skulker, normally seen around bamboo growth and is loathe to ascend the upper branches of trees. This dull-coloured bird has a rich, melodious voice and a wonderful repertoire of calls. It is most vocal during its breeding season between May and August.

Lithograph reproduced with the kind permission of the Bombay Natural History Society

The loud and cacophonous four-noted call of the Grey Junglefowl (above) can often be heard in the park in early mornings when the bird is more frequently sighted. Shy and wary, the cock has a sickle-shaped tail. Together with his sombre mate, he can be seen in clearings and on forest paths, digging for shoots, berries and insects. While the park's Grey Junglefowl population is still relatively good, their numbers seem to be on the decline over the past few years. The presence of this bird can serve as a yardstick for ascertaining the health of our forested regions.

During winter, the grass-encrusted, rocky terrain around Kanheri Caves is the favourite haunt of nightjars. Four species of these birds have been observed in the park. Very few Grey Nightjars stay behind to breed during summer. Supremely camouflaged, these cryptic-coloured birds (above left) are among the most difficult of wildlife to locate. During the day, they rest on grass and scrub-covered rocks, taking off on their insect-catching safaris around dusk (left). Each species of nightjar has its own distinct call which helps in identifying them.

Of the nine species of amphibians in the forest, the Fungoid Frog is one of the most colourful. It can be seen on the forest floor, rock-faces and occasionally on trees. During the dry months it gravitates towards water sources like the small water tank at the Conservation Education Centre of the BNHS (above). Like other amphibians, this brightly-coloured frog also breeds in the first half of the monsoon, laying eggs in shallow pools of water. It is popularly named Fungoid because of the reddish colouring on its back that resembles the Red Bark Fungus on certain forest trees.

In the early days of the monsoon, the 'rolling' croak of the Common Asian Toad (above right) was once a familiar sound near streams and puddles. Since the early-1990s, this stout-bodied amphibian has become less visible. With vocal sacs fully inflated, male toads broadcast their presence from exposed mounds and rocks, attracting neighbouring females. In their frantic search for a mate, when females are few and far between, the boisterous, libidinous males scramble towards them, forming a mass of clasping, pushing toads, appropriately termed 'toad-ball'. The Short-headed Burrowing Frog is a supreme example of camouflage (right). Rather toad-like in appearance, with a squat build and a warty skin, this frog is not particularly water-loving. It has spade-like appendages on its heels and it burrows backward into the soil.

Herpetologist, Vijay Awsare, first located the rare Forest Spotted Gecko (above) in the park in 1994. Previously found only in parts of India's southern peninsula, this was one of the earliest recorded sightings of the elusive reptile so far north. In June 2000, another specimen of this small, wonderfully patterned lizard was discovered here. Little is known about this reptile except that it is a nocturnal, ground gecko that lives on ants, termites and other small insects. Its presence in this easily accessible wilderness indicates that there is still much to be discovered in the park.

In the dark, old tunnel in the catchment area of Tulsi Lake, and in Kanheri Caves, the Rock Gecko (left) skulks secretively and sluggishly. Its appearance is exquisite – a large, broad-tailed reptile, beautifully spotted with dark markings on a pale buff and grey body, the spots and bands highly variable in individual animals. This lizard is chiefly insectivorous, perhaps also feeding on smaller lizards.

Predator and prey are at par with each other in nature's impartial game of survival. In the lush monsoon herbage of the countryside around Mumbai, a Common Green Whip Snake comes close to another hunter, a female Forest Calotes (top). So close and yet wonderfully hidden, the snake lies absolutely still. Then, very slowly, it creeps to within striking range, lashes out, and in a split-second grabs the stunned lizard. Holding the lizard in this position for about half a minute (above), the vine-like snake retreats into the shelter of the undergrowth. Usually entwined around thin, leafy branches, this well-known, bright green snake is very difficult to detect and is usually chanced upon by accident.

In the floral rhapsody of the monsoon, nature feasts and procreates, and myriad predators make the most of opportunities. Amid the low herbage, wrapped around bamboo and Karvi growth, the usually lethargic Green or Bamboo Pit Viper waits in ambush (left), its grass-green colour blending with the surroundings. It curves its lissom body, stubbornly securing itself to a leafy branch with its tail, to attain a striking pose.

Thrifty nature recycles everything. An army of ants discovers a dead Deccan Banded Gecko (above) on the park's main road. While ants are known to overpower prey much larger than themselves, it is doubtful that they killed this lizard. Slowly but resolutely and with impeccable coordination typical to ants, they shift the stocky reptile to a safer place to dismember it for consumption.

One monsoon morning, on the rocks around Kanheri Caves, I saw a Green Keelback take almost an hour and a half to completely swallow a big toad (left). Large prey is difficult to find and snakes can sometimes get so engrossed in devouring it that they may become quite unaware of their surroundings, making it possible to observe them at close quarters.

The most familiar animal in the park is also its most secretive. The Leopard (left), one of India's large cats, is a highly adaptable animal. This spotted feline, an expert tree-climber (above left) that moves silently across the forest floor, can be seen in the interiors of the forest as well as in the peripheral areas. Observations and surveys clearly suggest that many of these large cats live on the fringes of the forest, feeding largely on pariah-dogs. During summer, pug marks of leopards and digging signs of Sambar (above right) can often be seen around waterholes in the park.

One of India's most revered animals, the Common Langur or Hanuman Monkey normally keeps to the forested, central tracts of the park, sometimes straying into the fringes. Their troop size is not very large and at the most ten animals can be seen on their favoured feeding trees, like the flowering Flame of the Forest. It is sometimes sighted along with the more widespread Bonnet Macaque. These arboreal langurs often descend to the forest floor in the course of their search for feeding sites (above). It is among the earliest and most reliable of forest animals that caution other animals of leopard movement. Many leopard sightings have been made by heeding the staccato warning cries of this monkey.

The Bonnet Macaque (above right) is the most common species of monkey in the park and its troops may contain as many as thirty animals. They can be seen regularly around Kanheri Caves, attracted by easy pickings of food brought into the forest by picnickers. In high-density tourist areas, this macaque has become a tame but bold creature, often snatching food from the hands of visitors. The third primate found in the park is the Rhesus Macaque which is not an original inhabitant of this area. Easily identifiable by its short tail and bright, reddish-orange loins and rump (right), these monkeys have established themselves in the park after being released in small numbers over the years.

Open stretches around Vihar Lake are often visited by small herds of Spotted Deer. The population of these ungulates had reached an all-time low in the late-1960s and small numbers have been released since then with a view to re-establishing them. This fine-looking deer (above) keeps to the lower, shaded tracts, often around the lakes where moderate-sized herds of around forty animals can be encountered.

The Sambar (right) usually keeps to the hilly areas though it has to regularly visit the low-lying waterholes or lakes. Usually, this impressive deer remains either solitary or roams in small herds of not more than six animals. It is extremely wary and bolts at the slightest sign of intrusion, sometimes with a loud alarm call. Both Spotted Deer and Sambar can be seen occasionally near the park's main road.

PEOPLE
AND THE
FOREST

Surrounded by the expanding suburbs of Mumbai, the Sanjay Gandhi National Park is a tropical forest housing a varied plant and animal life. "Mumbai's national park is a refreshing escape from the scramble of India's commercial capital," says Vinod Haritwal, executive director of a chemicals and engineering corporation. From his impressive office in the northern suburb of Kandivli, the park's hills are clearly visible as is the continuously altering skyline of north Mumbai. Sky-rocketing apartment towers outside the park rival sprawling shanty towns that sometimes encroach upon forest lands.

Many people who come to the park for nature walks, morning strolls and photography, echo similar sentiments. "Where else can you dream of encountering a wild peafowl or chance upon some elusive wildlife shortly before reaching your office?" asks an effervescent lawyer who walks nearly four kilometres every day. On a morning walk with a colleague he once came within 10 m of a leopard. A couple of hours later he was in his south Mumbai office. "My colleague never accompanied me for another morning stroll after that," he says with a laugh.

Some time ago, at a social gathering, a discussion centred on the paucity of open spaces in cities. Someone drew a parallel between New York and Mumbai, whereupon Barbara Lornie, who works with an international airline and sometimes travels to the USA, remarked, "There is one huge difference between the two cities; New York has Central Park but there isn't anything like it in Mumbai." It is true that downtown Mumbai is awfully congested, though it has its sprinkling of public grounds. Much of suburban Mumbai is even worse. But the city has a national park – a real tropical wilderness spread over a large area, I informed Barbara. A couple of weeks later, Barbara sighted over thirty species of birds on their first visit to this forest.

More people live in the immediate vicinity of the park than around any other protected area in India. "Rapid urbanisation in and around Mumbai is exerting tremendous biotic pressure on the fringes of the park," says Suresh Gairola, Conservator, Wildlife. Though some people, knowingly or unknowingly, cause harm to the forest there are others who are concerned about its survival. The great ornithologist, Humayun Abdulali, played a crucial role in getting this forest declared a protected area during his tenure as Honorary Secretary of the Bombay Natural History Society (BNHS) in the 1950s and 1960s. The biodiversity and accessibility of this park has ensured that people remain interested in the natural world. An increasing number of city-dwellers are becoming aware of environmental issues. The media discusses and reports on these issues. Policy-makers know there is an environmentally conscious populace whose concerns cannot be ignored. Yet, conserving this wilderness continues to be a challenging and complex task.

TOP: *A stretch of Dahisar river, just outside the park, overflowing with sewage and industrial waste.*

BOTTOM: *High-rise apartments, slums, quarries, form a menacing foreground to the park's peripheral western hills.*

Are people the bane of this park? I do not think so. Perhaps the inability of environmentalists to reach out to a majority of people and sensitise them to the true worth of this wilderness has something to do with their indifference. Maybe it is our unimaginative approach and the lack of nature education for children that stifles their inborn love for the wild. This continuing

isolation from our environment only serves to widen the chasm between people and nature. The average city-dweller has no time and is simply struggling to survive like the half a million people inhabiting the immediate periphery of the park. With such large numbers living near the forest, encroachment becomes a continual problem. Removing encroachers from forest lands has snowballed into a major issue and the Bombay High Court has given a momentous judgement in favour of evicting them, subject to their suitable resettlement.

The Bombay Environment Action Group (BEAG) has been at the helm of environmental affairs in the Mumbai region, which includes the park, for many years. "The magnitude of the problem can be gauged by the fact that in an area where entry without permit is illegal, over a quarter of a million people were residing inside park lands until recently," says Debi Goenka, an activist of BEAG. "Fortunately, after an uphill litigation that began in 1995, BEAG has obtained strong orders from the Bombay High Court; all commercial activities inside the park have been stopped and encroachments have to be removed in a time-bound fashion. An area of about 180 hectares has already been restored to the park and habitat improvement activities have already begun on about 60 hectares," he adds. Goenka has vowed to continue the fight for the protection of this forest.

While for the people living on its fringes the park lands are just wild growth, for a considerable number they offer a revitalising haven of escape after a week of toil. On Sunday afternoons, the park's tourism zone has thousands of visitors. People usually go for a trek, visit Kanheri Caves and spend the afternoon boating, riding on the mini-train or visiting the tiger and lion safaris. Nearly 10,000 people visit the park daily and as many as 40,000 people come here on some weekends between October and March. "With nearly two million visitors annually, this must be India's most visited national park. Though the high influx of people exerts tremendous pressure on the habitat, it provides an excellent opportunity for generating an awareness and concern for nature," observes Gairola. A R Bharati, the Deputy Conservator in charge of the park agrees, "The easy accessibility of this park provides a unique opportunity for people to experience the aims and objectives of national parks in general, and helps create a healthy public opinion for the promotion of outdoor values."

Like many other protected areas Mumbai's national park is divided into two distinct parts, the aim being to promote recreation and tourism and protect its wildlife simultaneously. Krishnagiri Upavan, an area of 866 hectares towards the northern gate at Borivli, has been set aside as the tourism zone. It is dominated by a hillock on which stands a domed memorial of Mahatma Gandhi, probably the most prominent landmark of the park. The mini-train, gardens, deer park, lion and tiger safaris and boat rides, all lie in this zone. "We are vigorously trying to promote the concept of ecotourism here, as against mere recreational tourism that has generally been in vogue," Gairola explains. "Considering the significance of ecotourism as a means of conservation, it is imperative that it be handled and promoted carefully," advises Bharati whose proposed action plan for tourism emphasises nature education, habitat improvement and the development of a core team of resource personnel.

TOP: *A Mumbai local train cuts through the congested suburbs near the park.*

BOTTOM: *A group of children on a visit to the park.*

Until recently, the famous Mumbai snack, *bhelpuri*, was available inside the park's tourism zone. Food and tea stalls have now been banned and removed following a court order leaving many elated as they were filth-generating, shabby shacks. But banning and closure might not be the best option. Today, people carry food into the park littering the forest with plastic bags, cans and tetrapacks. In a tourism zone, select, well-managed eateries can be an asset. After all, the very purpose of a demarcated tourism zone is to ensure that the larger nature reserve area remains relatively undisturbed.

While the small tourism zone restricts the flow of visitors into the protected nature reserve zone, tremendous pressure continues to be exerted along the park's peripheral tracts. Along stretches of scrubby hillsides bordering the park, a tussle for land carries on between people and the forest. The rising shanty towns are wreaking havoc on areas that need protection, resulting in a nightmare not just for the city but the forest too.

Extensive encroachments dominate the fringes of the park and some of the hillsides have been brutally mauled. In an extraordinarily brazen display of 'might is right', Sheikh Quarry, one of the largest quarries, was operational on a whopping 25 hectares until recently; a travesty of the well-intentioned acquisition of land for the park. Fortunately, due to the proactive involvement of the forest department and several non-government organisations like the BEAG, the courts ordered its closure. These devastated stretches have once again come under the protection of the forest department.

The huge sprawl of Sheikh Quarry lies close to the Dahisar entry point to Mumbai. Today, its landscape resembles an abandoned mining town movie set, the massive machinery lying, as if fossilised. The terrain is unnaturally rugged, fashioned by more than two decades of blasting. Against the backdrop of an ever-expanding city, the cliff-like formations and the teak plantations make a strange sight. Habitat improvement measures are under way. The abandoned and desolate Sheikh Quarry is a giant symbol of effective positive action.

In some areas, people living on the park's fringes trespass into the forest along a network of narrow trails. Carrying out logs of timber and firewood, the trespassers often have an easy access due to the absence of a boundary wall along the park's periphery. Except for certain priority zones, most of the park remains without a perimeter fencing and it is not very difficult to enter this peerless wilderness. "Presently, only a 4.5 km long boundary wall exists though nearly 22 km has been identified as a priority stretch, along the western and eastern periphery," informs A R Bharati.

People from surrounding shanty towns also infiltrate the forest area for brewing illicit liquor. Until recently, these primitive distilleries were the source of pollution in various streams during the monsoon, the preferred season for this clandestine activity. Illegally chopped trees served as fuel for brewing liquor, emitting a putrid effluvium. Though not entirely eradicated, distilling is on the decline. All the same, adequate security is required to prevent its resurgence and the existing pattern of patrolling needs to be urgently reviewed.

In most of India's protected areas, an inadequately equipped staff continues to be a problem. Some of the personnel trained for forest and wildlife jobs in this park are diverted to supervising tourist activity, affecting the security and administration of the park. This spectacular wilderness deserves more than a cursory regard. It is imperative that the concerned authorities realise that by making a reasonable investment, the park could yield returns, both educational and financial, much beyond its present levels, resulting in its better management and protection.

Dedicated efforts of some people spell hope for devastated tracts like Sheikh Quarry.

The most volatile problem faced by the park today is leopards straying outside its limits. People on the fringes of the park and thousands of encroachers still living within this forest, occasionally come into accidental conflict with this spotted creature. The existence of the leopard in Mumbai's national park, surrounded by a sea of humanity, has raised a multitude of disturbing questions. For over a decade, leopards have been increasingly sighted in peripheral areas of the forest. Over thirty people have been killed in the last thirteen years by leopards in the park's areas that fall in the municipal limits of Mumbai and Thane.

A reconnaissance of the slums around the forest reveals that the leopard threat is real. I walk through the Lahugad and Ramnagar slums that proliferate adjacent to the prestigious, newly-built residential complexes at Kandivli, not far from the sprawling plant of India's largest manufacturer of jeeps and tractors. Vijay Awsare, alert and quick as ever, locates fresh pug marks of a leopard, and minutes later, a recent scat, perhaps an hour old. We see signs of the cat's presence along the Shankar Tekdi and Rahul Nagar hutments near Bhandup, on the park's eastern side. "It has made life miserable for us; we cannot go out after dark," laments a resident, who lost a close friend to a leopard attack. For the people living in the many hamlets inside the forest, the leopard is a constant worry.

I visit the Chunapada hamlet, a cluster of twenty-five huts in the forest, barely a couple of hundred metres off the main road leading to Kanheri Caves. It was here that four-year-old Rekha was fatally mauled by a leopard in 1987, perhaps the earliest of leopard attacks in the park. In this very hamlet, in the early hours of October 5, 1999, 29-year-old Vasant Soni Kharvu was killed by a leopard. Two months later, the death toll mounted, as Barkya Gangurde, a 70-year-old man, was attacked by a leopard on the night of December 4. The proposal to relocate the hamlets seems to have reached an impasse.

In the areas within and outside the park, the leopard is probably drawn to human settlements by the presence of domestic dogs, goats and poultry. The astute carnivore's behaviour is perhaps predictable because of a small natural prey base and the lack of a wide corridor or link to any extensive adjoining wilderness. Domestic animals are easy prey and in its quest the leopard occasionally comes into direct conflict with people. Ravi Chellam and Advait Edgaonkar, researchers at the Wildlife Institute of India, believe that as there is insufficient wild ungulate prey for the park's leopards, domestic dogs constitute their principal prey. According to them, "Though it may appear that the leopards are unlikely to ever face a shortage of this (domestic dog) prey, and this could probably be one of the reasons for the unusually high density of leopards here, it is doubtful if these dogs will continue to be their predominant prey. A disease or an epidemic could well wipe out the dog population in this region."

Over the past few years, there have been many leopard sightings outside the park. An abandoned cub was found in a residential complex. Several automobile drivers on the busy Ghodbunder Road have come across leopards at night and even during the day on a couple of occasions. The presence of a leopard once held up the shooting of a film in the government-run film studio complex just off the park's southern boundary. A leopard once boarded a Mumbai public transport bus at a regular bus stop in the crowded suburban area near the Holy Spirit Hospital at Andheri. The distraught driver and the few bleary-eyed, early-morning passengers bolted. When I reached the spot, an hour and a half later, the police and the fire brigade had arrived,

A warning sign indicating the presence of leopards in the park.

attracting a huge crowd of curious, frightened and frenzied onlookers. The young leopard had managed to hide under the bus by clambering on to the front axle. It took three hours before the park's Veterinary Officer, Dr R P Barhate, managed to tranquillise the leopard by using a rudimentary blow-dart.

A few days later, on March 12, 1992, another leopard was sighted, barely half a kilometre from the spot where the leopard had boarded the bus. It was early morning, and the young cat was seen loitering near Gyan Ashram, a cultural institute. By the time the fire brigade and the park's personnel arrived, the lissom cat, evidently much disturbed, found refuge in a tall, densely-foliaged mango tree. What followed was a four-hour ordeal as efforts were made to get the disturbed and aggressive leopard to climb down. Finally, Dr Barhate climbed to the top of a collapsible ladder raised from one of the fire brigade vans. His vivid green blow-dart once again came to the rescue.

When incidents like this occur, damaging backlash against wildlife and conservation are to be expected. Of almost a hundred incidents of leopard attacks that have been reported since 1986-87, inside and outside the park, more than thirty have resulted in human casualty. Over three-fourths of the victims have been children.

Some years ago, a young leopard was stoned to death in a shanty town near Bhandup, on the park's eastern fringes. An adult leopard was found dead on the park's periphery on the day Barkya Gangurde was killed by a leopard at Chunapada. Angry residents of hutments on the park's periphery say that they have nothing against leopards but, "if any incident of mauling recurs, we will retaliate and get rid of the animals. Our lives are more precious than wildlife". With more and more people settling here, the matter has assumed alarming proportions. In just the past two years, five leopards have been found dead under suspicious circumstances.

Official census estimates projected the park's leopard population at nearly forty in the late 1990s. Sceptics wonder whether the leopard population here has actually risen that much and are wary about the authenticity of the census figures. "In the light of figures for the available prey population, this park may have a crude density of as high as one leopard for every 2.4 sq km, which is surprising," assert Ravi Chellam and Advait Edgaonkar. "However, the crude density is estimated using only the designated area of the park. Considering that leopards here extensively frequent areas outside the park, the actual figure and density can be very different though at present we have no objective way of ascertaining the exact area used by the leopard outside the park," says Ravi Chellam. Do the frequent reports of the cat's presence in the vicinity of human settlements present a misleading picture, or is there truly such a shortage of natural prey in the park?

How accurate are the census figures for wildlife? "Every year, we conduct a population estimate of leopards and other wildlife," Gairola informs. "The pug mark of each individual leopard is distinct and an analysis gives a fair idea of the population trend; the plaster-casts are carefully investigated by experts to rule out any possibility of duplication. While the camera-trap technique may be more reliable for ascertaining the presence of individual animals, it may not be of much help in arriving at an accurate estimate of the total number of animals in an area. It is also more time-consuming and expensive and requires a higher degree of expertise. Finally, it must be kept in mind that no population estimation technique for wildlife can be foolproof and totally accurate even though these estimations help wildlife managers to decide on the various management interventions required," he elaborates.

A captured leopard is released into the park.

Some suggest that one solution to minimising people-animal interaction on the park's outskirts is to keep the area clean. This will control the population of scavenging domestic animals, thus reducing the attraction of the peripheral areas. "But where is the sizeable ungulate population that can keep all the leopards inside the forest? Management of this area demands different approaches and while current problems of high urgency have to be addressed, there are important issues that need technical understanding," K N Khawarey, Deputy Conservator, Management Plan, points out. "One such issue is related to biological fragmentation. The major part of the park, south of Bassein Creek, is surrounded by urban settlements and forms what is known as a fenced island. If proper management techniques are not employed, this fragmentation could, over a period of time, lead to a biodiversity reduction – a problem often compounded by human interests in conflict with nature. It is unlikely that the strategy of protective locking away of resources could work here," he says.

Another important task is to identify animals that require urgent conservation. Does blanket protection always work, especially in such an island-like protected area? Do all leopards require to be protected or would it be more desirable to systematically maintain their wild population so as to minimise their conflict with people? Technology may hold the answers to the accurate identification of individual animals, to estimating population trends and so much more, but sympathy and sensitivity too are required to maintain the delicate balance between human interests and the survival of the wilderness.

The conflict between people and animals can only be reduced, never completely eliminated. According to A R Bharati, "A solid boundary wall was to be constructed in some areas but since there were some existing encroachments, we put up a chain-link fence for a 4.5 km stretch to prevent further encroachments. Habitat restoration work is in progress on about 60 hectares of heavily encroached land that was reverted a couple of years ago to the forest department following a court order."

As I stand atop the dark rocks of Kanheri, struggling with this quintessential problem, I am increasingly convinced that the current desperate times demand drastic measures – the creation of a physical divide to prevent encroachments into the forest. Today, India's protected area has been reduced to about three percent of its total area, with much of this too under grave threat. Mumbai's national park needs to be conserved as urgently as many other protected areas in the country. Technological help and corporate support will be required to prevent further fragmentation of the park.

With Mumbai having the distressing distinction of being one of the most polluted and crowded cities in the world, this forest is its only salvation. Every visit here is magical – so apparent in the joyful faces of the underprivileged and handicapped children from local institutions who come here on nature walks, sponsored by an international corporate. No sooner do the children step off the bus than an indescribable joy spreads over their faces. An effervescent Greater Racket-tailed Drongo greets them, joined by the loud crow of a lordly Grey Junglefowl. There cannot be a more inspiring place than the park for discovering the wonders of nature. This fragile web of life that has taken millions of years in creation is on the brink of destruction. Neglected much longer, the forest and its vault of natural wealth might be lost forever.

The increasing number of corporate houses taking an interest in environmental issues is a sign that all is not lost. Mumbai's national park offers a unique opportunity for private and public sectors – corporate houses, the municipal corporation, the departments of electricity and police and many others – to work together towards conserving our natural heritage.

People on a nature walk in the forest.

Until recently, a quarter of a million people resided inside the park. Thousands still live in shanty towns along the fringes of the park's hills, constantly impinging on this wilderness (above). After an uphill litigation, the Bombay Environment Action Group (BEAG) has obtained orders from the Bombay High Court for their time-bound removal. In the last two years nearly 50,000 encroaching hutments have been demolished from these areas.

Along the park's western and eastern peripheries the phenomenal transformation of suburban Mumbai's skyline is visible (left). The pressures from this burgeoning population are enormous, not just on the park but on the city as well.

Following a court order in 1997, a heavily encroached area of about 60 hectares was cleared of slums. Park authorities have undertaken habitat improvement measures on these lands with the help of local volunteers from schools, colleges and private organisations. In Gautam Nagar, an area adjoining the western suburb of Kandivli, nature is beginning to replace the debris of a demolished shanty town. Saplings of indigenous trees have been planted and de-weeding exercises are regularly carried out to ensure their survival (above). The subsequent, much larger demolition drive between March and June 2000 saw an additional 120 hectares of encroached lands cleared of hutments. But these measures are not enough. A more intense participation of the forest department, city people and private corporations is needed to restore these lands.

In an attempt to protect the recovered lands from further encroachments, a high chain-link fence has been erected (right) along a 4.5 km stretch of highly sensitive and vulnerable area on the park's fringes.

For almost two decades, illegal quarrying was brazenly carried out in some areas along the park's boundary (left). Close to the Western Express Highway, along the park's northern periphery near the suburban township of Dahisar, lies the 20-hectare-Sheikh Quarry (above left), its jagged landscape shaped by human action. In 1999, the courts ordered the closure of Sheikh Quarry. A surreal panorama of cliff-like formations, secondary bush growth and rain-filled depressions can be seen against the backdrop of Mumbai's ever-expanding suburbs. Recently, groups of people have helped in the construction of check-dams and contributed to other habitat improvement measures in Sheikh Quarry (above and top).

The easy access to the wealth of commercially exploitable animals and plants in the park has lead to illegal activities such as poaching and logging (above). The efficiency of patrolling inside and along the park's periphery has to be seriously reviewed if poaching is to be prevented and the forest freed from the ringing of the axe.

Nature is exceptionally resilient and given a fair chance the wilderness will flourish. In early March, a forest fire charred the land around Vihar Lake. Within a few days of the monsoon's arrival a carpet of profuse herbage covered the landscape. Even in this burnt tree-stump (right) a few frail blades of grass took root.

Leopards sometimes stray outside the park limits, onto highways and areas of human habitation (above, left and following pages). The forest office or the local fire brigade is usually called in to capture the animal, often a risky exercise. Thereafter, the leopard is either subjected to a life of captivity or is released back into the forest. At times, leopards straying into human territory on the park's outskirts meet with tragic consequences.

While it is important that people continue to visit the park, the damage they sometimes cause to its wildlife needs to be controlled. These images taken inside and around the park show the harm done to a vulnerable biodiversity – a snake run over by an automobile (top), a hyena shot dead at the edge of the forest (above left), a waterhen crushed on the road (above right).

The low population of wild ungulates in the forest, especially deer, has been cited as one of the reasons for leopards straying outside the park. With a view to replenish the ungulate population, the forest department and Mumbai's municipal corporation have released more than two hundred deer over the past decade. In 1999, during the Wildlife Week, twenty-one deer were released (above right and right). However, it is not clear if this exercise has helped reduce the conflict between people and leopards.

Mahashivratri, a festival venerating Lord Shiva, is celebrated in February or early March and it completely changes the face of Mumbai's national park. More than 2,00,000 people throng the park (above right) on their way to Kanheri Caves (above) and the Gomukh temple that lies 125 m above the caves. In recent years, volunteers have tried to cope with this frightening invasion. Despite their efforts, considerable stretches of the forest are swamped by garbage or damaged by fire (right).

Nearly half the people residing in the eleven unauthorised hamlets in the park are tribals belonging to the Warli, Koli and Thakur communities. Some of them are quite knowledgeable about the forest and its wildlife. This young tribal boy (above) seemed to have a fairly good idea about the birds in the park.

During the Ganesh Chaturthi festival, towards the end of the monsoon, idols of Ganesh, the elephant god (left), are immersed in a small pond and along an adjoining stretch of the Dahisar river in the park's tourism zone. Euphoric devotees swarm a short stretch of the narrow river to submerge hundreds of idols in its shallow waters. While the forest department and local police make arrangements for safe and trouble-free festivities, indifferent devotees leave their mark on the forest – the river can be seen overflowing with refuse the next morning (above left).

Mumbai is probably India's only metropolis that has an ancient Buddhist site. Lying within the folds of the park, Kanheri Caves date from the first century B.C. to the ninth century A.D. The word 'Kanheri' is derived from the Sanskrit term *krishnagiri* which means 'black mountain', an obvious reference to its dark, volcanic rocks (above left). There are 109 *viharas* or monk cells chiselled out of the rock, meant for residence and meditation. The location of these caves and the inscriptions found here (top) indicate that Kanheri was an important point on an ancient trade route in Western India. Cave No. 3 (left), the largest and architecturally the most elaborate cave, is adorned with various sculptures (above) including huge figures of Buddha. Grey Nightjar, Malabar Whistling Thrush, Dusky Crag Martin, Blacknaped Hare and several reptiles and bats find refuge in and around the caves, even as people continue to ravage these ancient relics. Human presence has already driven away a large colony of Fulvous Fruit-bats that once thrived in one of the caves.

The park, rich in wildlife and natural beauty, attracts thousands of people daily. Its beautiful landscape – the mangrove creek, rocky overhangs, shaded streams, freshwater wetlands – provides the right ambience for corporate houses who hold their management training programmes here (above). Wetland areas like those around Vihar Lake are an ideal spot for bird-watching (top), especially during winter. The large rock-face above Kanheri is a favourite site for rock-climbing (right).

The tiger safari, spread over 20 hectares, was inaugurated in 1998 and has become a major attraction in the park's tourism zone (above). Inside the safari enclosure tigers can be sighted amid dense growth and they sometimes emerge on forest trails.

Apartments overlooking some areas of the park have a spectacular prospect. Photographer, Anand Udeshi's twelfth story apartment (top) has an uninterrupted view of Mumbai's wilderness. "It soothes my senses," says Udeshi, who moved here from a crowded area of the city's western suburbs. He adds, "It was always my desire to live amid such verdant surroundings."

People visit this park for a variety of reasons (left) – a man meditates in the peaceful surroundings of the forest, a nature enthusiast, hidden amid the dry grass, keeps a lookout for birds and a poet finds inspiration along a secluded stream.

Towards the southern entrance of the park lies BNHS's Conservation Education Centre that spreads over 13 hectares of wilderness, near the sprawling Film City studio complex. The objective of this centre is to sensitise children and adults towards their environment (above), fostering an understanding and appreciation of the forest and its biodiversity.

The park is accessible to a large number of people living in and around Mumbai. At the edge of Vihar Lake, college students on a study tour to the park, listen in rapt attention to their instructor (above left). On the way to the park's highest point, BNHS members watch a herpetologist handle a snake just prior to releasing it in the forest (left).

The burgeoning population and its attendant need for more land and natural resources threatens the survival of the national park and its inhabitants. Continuing unabated it could destroy the fragile ecological balance crucial to our own survival. A protracted and combined effort can help preserve the balance in areas such as Mumbai's national park.

SPECIES LIST

Common Name	Scientific Name
AMPHIBIANS	
Common Asian Toad	*Bufo melanostictus*
Fungoid Frog	*Rana malabarica*
Indian Bull Frog	*Hoplobatrachus tigerinus*
Ornate Narrow-mouthed Frog	*Microhyla ornata*
Short-headed Burrowing Frog	*Tomopterna breviceps*
BIRDS	
Ashy Prinia (Ashy Wren-Warbler)	*Prinia socialis*
Asian Openbill (Openbill Stork)	*Anastomus oscitans*
Banded Bay Cuckoo	*Cacomantis sonneratii*
Baya Weaver	*Ploceus philippinus*
Black Kite	*Milvus migrans*
Black Redstart	*Phoenicurus ochruros*
Black-capped Kingfisher	*Halcyon pileata*
Black-headed Gull	*Larus ridibundus*
Black-headed Ibis (White Ibis)	*Threskiornis melanocephalus*
Black-hooded Oriole	*Oriolus xanthornus*
Black-naped Monarch (Blacknaped Blue Flycatcher)	*Hypothymis azurea*
Black-shouldered Kite	*Elanus caeruleus*
Blue Rock Thrush	*Monticola solitarius*
Bluethroat	*Luscinia svecica*
Booted Eagle	*Hieraaetus pennatus*
Brahminy Kite	*Haliastur indus*
Bronze-winged Jacana	*Metopidius indicus*
Brown Fish Owl	*Ketupa zeylonensis*
Brown Hawk Owl	*Ninox scutulata*
Brown-cheeked Fulvetta (Quaker Babbler)	*Alcippe poioicephala*
Common Hawk Cuckoo	*Hierococcyx varius*
Common Hoopoe	*Upupa epops*
Common Myna	*Acridotheres tristis*
Common Stonechat	*Saxicola torquata*
Common Tailorbird	*Orthotomus sutorius*
Crested Serpent Eagle	*Spilornis cheela*
Crimson Sunbird (Yellowbacked Sunbird)	*Aethopyga siparaja*
Dusky Crag Martin	*Hirundo concolor*
Emerald Dove	*Chalcophaps indica*
Eurasian Marsh Harrier	*Circus aeruginosus*
Golden-fronted Leafbird (Goldfronted Chloropsis)	*Chloropsis aurifrons*
Great Hornbill	*Buceros bicornis*
Greater Racket-tailed Drongo	*Dicrurus paradiseus*
Green Sandpiper	*Tringa ochropus*
Grey Heron	*Ardea cinerea*
Grey Junglefowl	*Gallus sonneratii*
Grey Nightjar (Jungle Nightjar)	*Caprimulgus indicus*
Grey Wagtail	*Motacilla cinerea*
Grey-bellied Cuckoo (Plaintive Cuckoo)	*Cacomantis passerinus*
Grey-breasted Prinia (Franklin's Wren-Warbler)	*Prinia hodgsonii*
Grey-headed Fish Eagle	*Ichthyophaga ichthyaetus*
House Crow	*Corvus splendens*
Indian Grey Hornbill	*Ocyceros birostris*
Indian Scimitar Babbler (Slaty-headed Scimitar Babbler)	*Pomatorhinus horsfieldii*
Jungle Owlet	*Glaucidium radiatum*
Laggar Falcon	*Falco jugger*
Large-billed Crow (Jungle Crow)	*Corvus macrorhynchos*
Lesser Whistling-duck (Lesser Whistling Teal)	*Dendrocygna javanica*
Little Cormorant	*Phalacrocorax niger*
Little Heron	*Butorides striatus*
Little Tern	*Sterna albifrons*
Long-tailed Shrike (Rufousbacked Shrike)	*Lanius schach*

Common Name	Scientific Name
Malabar Pied Hornbill	*Anthracoceros coronatus*
Malabar Whistling Thrush	*Myophonus horsfieldii*
Mottled Wood Owl	*Strix ocellata*
Oriental Honey-buzzard	*Pernis ptilorhyncus*
Oriental Magpie Robin	*Copsychus saularis*
Osprey	*Pandion haliaetus*
Painted Stork	*Mycteria leucocephala*
Pheasant-tailed Jacana	*Hydrophasianus chirurgus*
Pied Cuckoo (Pied Crested Cuckoo)	*Clamator jacobinus*
Plum-headed Parakeet (Blossomheaded Parakeet)	*Psittacula cyanocephala*
Puff-throated Babbler (Spotted Babbler)	*Pellorneum ruficeps*
Purple Heron	*Ardea purpurea*
Purple Sunbird	*Nectarinia asiatica*
Purple Swamphen (Purple Moorhen)	*Porphyrio porphyrio*
Red Spurfowl	*Galloperdix spadicea*
Red-wattled Lapwing	*Vanellus indicus*
Rufous Woodpecker	*Celeus brachyurus*
Shaheen (Peregrine) Falcon	*Falco peregrinus peregrinator*
Shikra	*Accipiter badius*
Slaty-breasted Rail (Bluebreasted Banded Rail)	*Gallirallus striatus*
Tickell's Blue Flycatcher	*Cyornis tickelliae*
Whiskered Tern	*Chlidonias hybridus*
White-bellied Sea Eagle	*Haliaeetus leucogaster*
White-eyed Buzzard	*Butastur teesa*
White-rumped Shama	*Copsychus malabaricus*
INSECTS	
Atlas Moth	*Attacus atlas*
Blue Mormon	*Papilio polymnestor*
Blue Oakleaf	*Kallima horsfieldi*
Common Blue Bottle	*Graphium sarpedon*
Crimson Rose	*Pachliopta hector*
Great Eggfly	*Hypolimnas bolina*
Harvester Ant	family *Formicidae**
Hawk Moth	family *Sphingidae**
Hitler Bug	*Catacanthus incarnatus*
Orchid Mantis	*Creobroter apicalis*
Owl Moth	*Erabus macrops*
Painted Grasshopper	*Poecilocera picta*
Painted Handmaiden Moth	*Euchromia polymena*
Red Silk Cotton Bug	family *Pyrrhocoridae**
Short-horned Grasshopper	family *Acrididae**
Spot Swordtail	*Pathysa nomius*
Stick Insect	family *Phasmatidae**
Tiny Grass Blue	*Zizeeria gaika*
Tussar Silk Moth	*Antheraea paphia*
Wild Silk Moth	family *Saturniidae**
MAMMALS	
Barking Deer	*Muntiacus muntjak*
Blacknaped Hare	*Lepus nigricollis*
Bonnet Macaque	*Macaca radiata*
Common Langur, Hanuman Monkey	*Presbytis entellus*
Common Palm Civet	*Paradoxurus hermaphroditus*
Fourhorned Antelope	*Tetracerus quadricornis*
Fulvous Fruit-bat	*Rousettus leschenaulti*
Indian Bison, Gaur	*Bos gaurus*
Leopard	*Panthera pardus*
Rhesus Macaque	*Macaca mulatta*
Sambar	*Cervus unicolor*
Spotted Deer, Chital	*Axis axis*
Tiger	*Panthera tigris*

Common Name	Scientific Name
PLANTS	
Birthwort	*Aristolochia indica*
Commelina	*Commelina* sp.*
Costus, Spiral Ginger	*Costus speciosus*
Garden Balsam	*Impatiens balsamina*
Habenaria Orchid	*Habenaria longicorniculata*
Hill Turmeric	*Curcuma pseudomontana*
Karvi	*Carvia callosa*
Malabar Glory Lily	*Gloriosa superba*
Milkweed	*Calotropis gigantea*
Morning Glory	*Ipomoea pupurea*
Pink-striped Trumpet Lily	*Crinum* sp.*
Red Bark Fungus*	
Sensitive Smithia	*Smithia sensitiva*
Sesame	*Sesamum indicum*
Silver-spiked Cockscomb	*Celosia argentea*
Solid Bamboo	*Dendrocalamus strictus*
Thorny Bamboo	*Bambusa arundinacea*
Water Lettuce	*Pistia stratiotes*
REPTILES	
Common Green Whip Snake	*Ahaetulla nasutus*
Common Ratsnake	*Ptyas mucosus*
Deccan Banded Gecko	*Geckoella dekkanensis*
Forest Calotes	*Calotes rouxi*
Forest Spotted Gecko	*Geckoella collegalensis*
Green Keelback	*Macropisthodon plumbicolor*
Green or Bamboo Pit Viper	*Trimeresurus gramineus*
Indian Chameleon	*Chamaeleon zeylanicus*
Olivaceous Keelback	*Atretium schistosum*
Rock Gecko	*Hemidactylus maculatus*
Russell's Viper	*Vipera russelli*
SPIDERS & OTHERS	
Crab Spider	family *Thomisidae**
Giant Wood Spider	*Nephila maculata*
Red Velvet Mite	*Trombiculids**
Wolf Spider	family *Lycosidae**
TREES	
Ashoka	*Saraca asoca*
Black Plum	*Syzygium cumini*
Bonfire Tree	*Firmiana colorata*
Ceylon Oak	*Schleichera oleosa*
Flamboyant Flame Tree	*Delonix regia*
Flame of the Forest	*Butea monosperma*
Haldu	*Haldina cordifolia*
Indian Coral Tree	*Erythrina variegata*
Indian Jujube	*Ziziphus mauritiana*
Indian Kino Tree	*Pterocarpus marsupium* var. *acuminata*
Indian Laburnum	*Cassia fistula*
Iron Wood Tree	*Memecylon umbellatum*
Karaya	*Sterculia urens*
Laurel	*Terminalia crenulata*
Mango Tree	*Mangifera indica*
Pongam Oil Tree	*Pongamia pinnata*
Red Silk Cotton	*Bombax ceiba*
Strangler Fig	*Ficus* spp.*
Teak	*Tectona grandis*
Wild Guava	*Careya arborea*
Wild Hog Plum	*Spondias acuminata*

Note: The bird names in brackets are the more familiar names.
* Insufficient information available regarding genus and species identification.

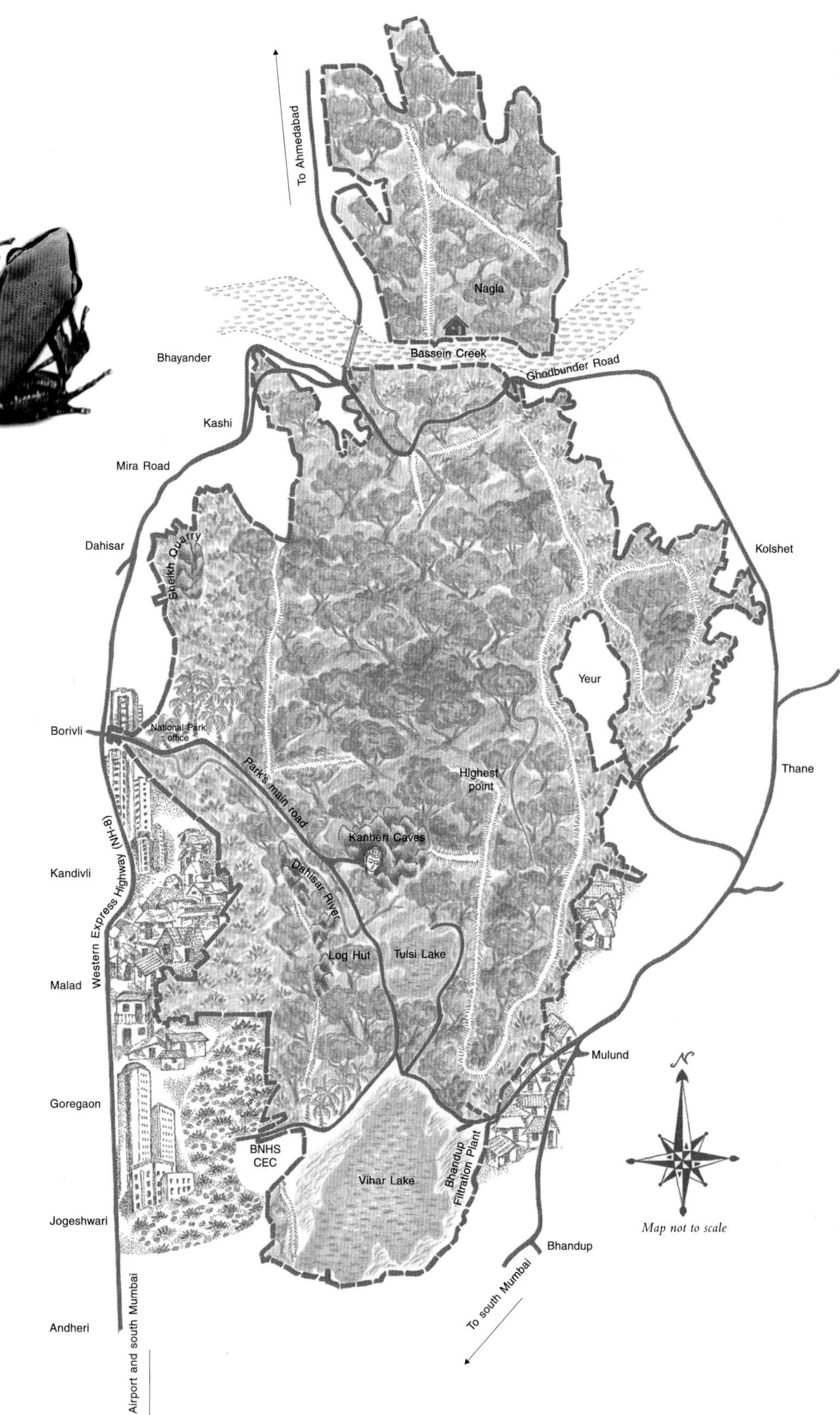

SANJAY GANDHI NATIONAL PARK

INDEX

ACKNOWLEDGEMENTS

I thank my parents, Ravin Monga and Dr G S Monga for introducing me to the magical world of this forest. My father's comments on the manuscript were invaluable. My wife, Jyoti, continuously tolerated my passion, even encouraged it over the years; she was as much a part of it all as I. My family has been a constant source of inspiration, helping me make a profession of what initially seemed a pastime.

I sincerely thank the management of the Godrej group of companies for believing in the project and, yet again, for demonstrating their genuine commitment to environmental care.

The Maharashtra state forest department has been a helpful partner in this endeavour. I thank M G Gogate, former CCF (WL), Maharashtra, Suresh Gairola, CF (WL) and A K Nigam, CF (WL) for valuable guidance; A R Bharati, DCF – National Park for rendering all possible help; K N Khawarey, DCF (Management Plan) offered effective insight; DCFs Viswas Walke, S D Sathe and Nitin Kakodar were supportive at all times and I have spent many meaningful hours with them in this forest; Veterinary Officer Dr R P Barhate, ACFs R P Pakhare, S G Fale, N S Ladkat, Anil Anjankar, N B Bhure and K P Rao, and RFOs S B Gopale, Sameer Deshpande and Sanjay Chavan were there whenever I needed them. Grateful thanks are also due to many other officials of the forest department with whom I have interacted over the years.

I am much indebted to Humayun Abdulali, my 'guru', for a decade of highly rewarding bird-watching, and for writing the foreword. My long association with the BNHS helped me develop an intimate bond with the wild and I thank the BNHS for permission to use the Grey Junglefowl lithograph. The diligent Naira Ahmadullah for her many suggestions and for the map. Bittu Sahgal for enlightening me with a different, wider perspective on environment. The botanist M R Almeida for assistance in plant identification. Vinod Haritwal, Joslin Rodrigues, Sanal Nair and Vijay Awsare for always being around, a very special thanks. Manisha Shah, Andrea Britto, Kiran Srivastav, Rishad Naoroji, Nitin Jamdar, Dr Neil Soares, Ritul Mehta, Celine Anthony, Digant Desai, Major Madhav Mhaskar, Ulhas Rane, Anand Udeshi, Abhishek Salian and the delightful Hasu for wonderful moments in this forest – moments of joy, surprise and discovery.

I thank the unflinching Debi Goenka of the BEAG with whom my best wishes lie. Naresh Chaturvedi, Isaac Kehimkar, Prashant Mahajan, V Shubhalaxmi, Deepak Apte and Gayatri Ugra of the BNHS for species identification. I also thank Phillips Antiques for use of the Tiger in Salsette lithograph. The BMC's hydraulics department helped with useful data. The NRSA, Hyderabad graciously allowed me use of the FCC (satellite image). Dr Arun Inamdar of IIT, Mumbai for his comments on some sections of the book. Mr Samuel Israel read through the first draft of the manuscript and offered constructive suggestions. Mahesh Chaturvedi allowed me access to his management training workshops. I thank Gopal Bodhe, Krupakar-Senani, Anish Andheria, Thakur Dalip Singh, G V Ajay and Kedar Bhat for letting me use some of their images; Carl D'Silva for doing the bookmark illustration; the late J S Serrao for digging into a bit of history.

Padmini Mirchandani and Meera Ahuja at IBH, Shikha Gupta, the text editor, Sunil Mahadik, Shekhar Pitale and others at F X Designs. It was a strong publishing team and I owe it to your cooperation. Bharath Ramamrutham and Vinod Haritwal taught me the art of patience out of the forest. It paid.

Last but not least, I thank all the people who have helped this wonderful wilderness survive.

Photo Credits

Phillips Antiques: 14 (bottom); Krupakar-Senani: 51 (bottom), 52, 53 (bottom), 63 (centre), 94, 95, 99, 102; Gopal Bodhe: 39, 129, 146 (top); Anish Andheria: 82 (bottom), 113; Thakur Dalip Singh: 101 (bottom); BNHS: 105; G V Ajay: 114; Kedar Bhat: 126; Manisha Shah: Inside back flap.